SO-EKK-457

Conservation of Crop Germplasm—
An International Perspective

CSSA Special Publication Number 8

Proceedings of a symposium
sponsored by Divisions C-1, C-4, and A-6
of the Crop Science Society of America
in Washington, DC, 14–19 Aug. 1983.

Editorial Committee
W. L. Brown, Chm.
T. T. Chang
M. M. Goodman
Q. Jones

Managing Editor
David M. Kral

Associate Editor
Sherri H. Mickelson

1984
Published by the
CROP SCIENCE SOCIETY OF AMERICA
677 South Segoe Road
Madison, WI 53711

Cover Design: Julia M. Whitty

Copyright 1984 by the Crop Science Society of America.
ALL RIGHTS RESERVED UNDER THE U.S. COPYRIGHT
LAW OF 1978 (P.L. 94-553). Any and all uses beyond the
limitations of the "fair use" provision of the law require written
permission from the publisher(s) and/or the author(s); not
applicable to contributions prepared by officers or employees of
the U.S. Government as part of their official duties.

Crop Science Society of America
677 South Segoe Road, Madison, WI 53711 USA

Library of Congress Catalog Card Number: 84-72462.
Standard Book Number: 0-89118-518-6.

Printed in the United States of America

Table of Contents

Preface

Since the dawn of cultivation, man has created a myriad of crop forms which have provided a wealth of genetic diversity in most crop species. Yet an ever increasing world population, and the introduction of improved cultivars into the centers of crop diversity have caused serious erosion of much of the world's indigenous crop germplasm. The seriousness of this problem has received growing national and international attention, especially during the past 10 years. However, much remains to be done if the world's crop germplasm still extant is to be salvaged, properly conserved, and adequately utilized.

A symposium dealing with certain aspects of this subject was held at the 1983 Annual Meetings of the American Society of Agronomy. Jointly sponsored by Div. A-6, C-1, C-4, and the Committee on Preservation of Plant Germplasm of the Crop Science Society of America, the symposium consisted of six invited papers each of which is included in this publication. The subject matter ranged from a detailed description of the essential elements of successful plant exploration to the broadly defined goals, objectives, and operations of national (USA) and international (IBPGR) plant germplasm programs. Also described are the gene resource programs of two of the International Agricultural Research Centers, IRRI and ICRISAT. Germplasm conservation as practiced at the National Seed Storage Laboratory of the U.S. Department of Agriculture completes the series.

The information contained herein, gleaned from many years experience under a wide variety of geographic and political conditions, should be of interest to individuals and institutions engaged in any aspect of plant genetic resources. Certain of the papers should be of special interest to those institutions contemplating the development of new plant genetic resource centers.

Editorial Committee
W. L. Brown, Chairman
T. T. Chang
M. M. Goodman
Q. Jones

W. F. Keim, CSSA President

Chapter 1

Plant Exploration: Planning, Organization, and Implementation with Special Emphasis on *Arachis*[1]

C. E. SIMPSON[2]

When one considers the writings of the great plant explorers—O. F. Cook, David Fairchild, N. I. Vavilov, Walter T. Swingle, Frank N. Meyer, and others—in addition to the many well-known botanists who were their antecedents and contemporaries, it seems odd for an inconspicuous plant breeder, limited to one genus, to prepare a "how-to-do it" chapter on plant exploration. But times change as do the people who pursue the field work of germplasm collection. It is largely to the plant breeders, who must utilize the collections, that have fallen the duties of plant exploration, and it is to them and their administrative superiors that the remarks in this chapter will be addressed.

The subject matter implied by the title of this chapter and its illustration by the author's experience with *Arachis* L. will be applicable largely to the geographic areas and countries in South America where the work was conducted. It would be wishful to think that the problems presented to plant explorers in the Near East, Central China, Africa, or India, for example, would be resolved by the discussions presented in this chapter. Nevertheless, there is common ground to all plant exploration, introduction, and germplasm conservation.

[1] Contribution from the Texas Agric. Exp. Stn., Texas A&M Univ., College Station, TX. TA. no. 18947.

[2] Associate professor, Texas Agric. Exp. Stn., Texas A&M Univ., Stephenville, TX 76401.

Copyright © 1984 Crop Science Society of America, 677 South Segoe Road, Madison, WI 53711. *Conservation of Crop Germplasm—An International Perspective.*

It is the purpose of this chapter to bring forward some of the strengths of our program and to turn our weaknesses to the critical light of this forum and subsequently to the readers of its proceedings.

The collection and preservation of germplasm of cultivated crops and their wild relatives is recognized as an important aspect of plant breeding for improvement of commercial cultivars. Collection of crop species probably had its beginnings well before recorded history as hunters first became gatherers, and later cultivators as civilization advanced. Some of the earliest recorded expeditions for plant collections occurred around 1500 B.C. Even though numerous expeditions occurred in the early history of the New World, extensive collections were made after passage of the Morrill Act in 1862 (2), which resulted in a subsequent increase in agricultural research through the land-grant universities which the act established. Another significant factor at this time (1862) was the organization of the Department of Agriculture as a separate unit; and later (1898), the creation of the "Section of Foreign Seed and Plant Introduction" (5). Names which are synonymous to this era are Fairchild, N. E. Hansen, and Mark Carleton. It is important to point out that in many cases, the interest and drive of an individual scientist has contributed more to the crop collections than institutional and/or governmental programs.

As one would expect, and as it should have been, the major crops received attention first. Many lines of wheat (*Triticum aestivum* L. em Thell.), maize (*Zea mays* L.), cotton (*Gossypium* L. spp.), sorghum [*Sorghum bicolor* (L.) Moench], rice (*Oryza sativa* L.), potato (*Solanum tuberosum* L.), and other crops were collected during the first 60 years of the 20th century. Collections have come from three sources—primary centers of origin (Vavilov, cited from 5) or primary centers of diversity (8, 14); secondary centers of diversity; and/or sub-secondary centers.

The genus *Arachis* originated on the Southern Brazilian shield, probably well before a mid-Tertiary geologic uplift of the shield (11). Following a series of uplifts, the genus *Arachis* was dissected (along with the shield and lower peneplane) by downward moving soil and water. The evolution of the sections and species has occurred in the various major river valleys and their tributaries on the South American continent (11, 20). Running water has obviously played a major role in the distribution of the geocarpic *Arachis* species (11, 28). Gregory et al. (10) divided the genus into seven taxonomic sections and indicated the known areas (in 1973) of distribution of the sections. The known sectional distributions conformed geographically to certain river valleys or river valley systems. The South American region consists of the primary center of origin and diversity of *Arachis*. Krapovickas (21) described five secondary centers for cultivated peanut and Gregory et al. (10) added a sixth on the South American continent.

Hundreds of introductions of peanut (*A. hypogaea* L.) have come to the USA over the years in exchange programs (3), but it was not until 1959 (10) that intensive effort was made to collect wild species of *Arachis*. The efforts of Gregory, Krapovickas, and Pietrarelli, 1959 to 1967 (10), greatly increased the available wild and cultivated *Arachis* germplasm. Hammons and Langford (3, 10) added significant materials to the collection in 1968.

With concern over the genetic vulnerability of many crop plants (3, 8, 13, 15) a renewed international effort has been made to collect and preserve germplasm of all types. (Note: The 1975 Agronomy Abstracts (23) had 26 papers dealing with germplasm resources and genetic vulnerability of crop plants.) The Consultative Group on International Agricultural Research (CGIAR) and the Food and Agriculture Organization (FAO) of the United Nations (UN), through the International Board for Plant Genetic Resources (IBPGR), have become instrumental in many of these collection activities. (See other portions of this publication for IBPGR activities.) This chapter presents some guidelines for plant exploration planning and implementation using the collection of *Arachis* from December 1976 through May 1983 as a medium of illustration of the organization and execution of germplasm acquisition and conservation. The project was sponsored by IBPGR and supported in part by the agencies listed in Appendix I.

PLANNING

General. Planning for plant exploration expeditions must begin months or even years in advance of the actual trip(s). The first step in planning is the establishment of a consensus in the minds of scientific associates concerning the wisdom of acquiring the needed collections. Examples of this type of approach can be sited for several crops, including rice (6, 18), sorghum (25), and peanut (24). These documents resulted from international gatherings of scientists. More recently, several collection plans have been outlined by IBPGR (26, 27). Scientists interested in collection should become cognizant of the earlier activities of the national and international centers and IBPGR.

The second planning step is to provide the heads of the national and international agencies concerned, with the consensus, and to elicit from them the administrative support of a suggested proposal to request funds for acquiring germplasm materials. In the peanut program these agencies included IBPGR, International Crops Research Institute for the Semi-Arid Tropics (ICRISAT), U.S. Department of Agriculture (USDA), and the agencies of the several proposed cooperators (see Appendix I). Following the peanut germplasm workshop in Florida in 1975 (24), Gregory and Krapovickas corresponded with heads of several of these agencies in attempts to solicit interest and funds for *Arachis* exploration.

After administrative support from the several agencies is reasonably solid, step three should be initiated, i.e., the presentation to the appropriate agency of a closely reasoned proposal for the work, designating collaborating local scientists in the proposed area of collection, team members in the various countries, and a scheme for depositing collected materials in the home country, international research centers, and in the center of the researcher making the proposal.

In preparing the proposal, germplasm resources already collected and available need to be determined, as well as where additional re-

sources may be located. Primary and secondary centers of origin and/or
diversity need to be identified. For most major crops these areas have
been well documented, (8) but for certain minor crops this may not be
true.

A proposal for germplasm collection of peanut was submitted to the
IBPGR in January 1976 by Gregory and Krapovickas (12, 19). Subsequently, three additional proposals and revisions were submitted. Figure
1 shows the areas of proposed coverage by the various expeditions. The
first proposal was funded by IBPGR and the work began in November
1976.

Any potential plant explorer is encouraged to read the *IBP Handbook
No. 11, Genetic Resources in Plants* (8), and collection manuals prepared
by Chang et al. (7) and Hawkes (16, 17). These publications have a
wealth of pertinent information and will be of great benefit to a plant
collector.

Location. Detailed planning of an expedition begins with selection of
an area to be collected. Many factors can determine collection sites. It
may be advantageous to return to an area which has previously yielded

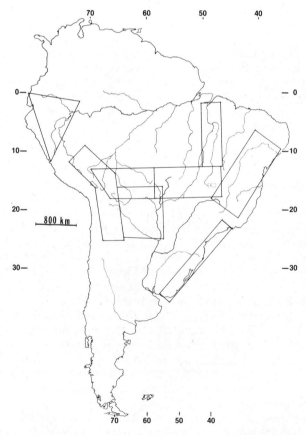

Fig. 1. Areas proposed to IBPGR for exploration for *Arachis*, 1976 to 1983.

genes for specific disease resistance. Perhaps a collection has proven particularly compatible as a parent, but lacks a specific character such as disease resistance; therefore, the area needs to be recollected. Further, specific collections may no longer be available in live germplasm banks. Various herbaria of the world contain specimens of wild species and may prove excellent sources of information for collection sites. Depending upon the crop being collected, it could prove useful to utilize Vavilov's centers of origin; however, for most species, more recent information is available (6, 8, 14). In the case of peanut, much of the older germplasm collections did not survive the introduction process; therefore, we were returning to acquire living materials. We also had potential collection sites based on the other sources mentioned above.

Team Concept. Team collection has definite advantages. The work load can be distributed according to each person's interests and capabilities. The amount of documentation of collections will vary with the capabilities of the team members. Thus, it is a good idea to comprise a team with varied backgrounds, but all with an interest in germplasm collection and preservation.

In planning for an expedition, care must be taken not to make a collection team too large. Funding may limit team size; however, the collection site can also place restrictions on the number of participants. If collections are to be made in a developing country, team size should probably not exceed four members, and ideally, only three. For example, if the only means of reaching a specific site is by single engine aircraft; a pilot, three team members, and a limited amount of collection gear will weigh 850 kg—the maximum load for common, small, fixed-wing aircraft. In addition, arrival of three extra mouths to feed in a remote village and the need for three more spaces to sleep is usually all that can be accommodated. Four or more people tend to "overload the system."

When roads and vehicles are available, four team members will be in order. A point of peak efficiency is reached at four; five or more give diminishing returns because time consumed in packing a vehicle or getting a meal prepared and eaten reaches a break-even point. Also, most vehicles will have adequate space for four plus their luggage, collection gear, and collections. More people will require a larger vehicle, which will likely not be available in most places.

It is extremely important in selecting a team to include a member from the country or state being collected. Also, it is advisable to try to locate local people to participate on a day to day basis. This may mean involving a local botanist or agronomist with only a passing interest in the goals of the expedition, but more often than not, these people contribute significantly to the success of a mission. In some countries with more advanced systems of agricultural research and/or germplasm preservation, local participation will be mandated by law.

The *Arachis* collection team, 1976 to 1983, initially included the three base members from the 1959, 1961, and 1967 expeditions: W. C. Gregory, A. Krapovickas, and J. Pietrarelli. From this nucleus the team(s) expanded to include C. E. Simpson, D. J. Banks, A. Schinini, H. Zurita O., and J. F. M. Valls (see Appendix I for professional affiliation of team

Table 1. Fate of wild *Arachis* introductions, 1936 to 1983.

Year of expedition(s)	Number collected	Number conserved	Until (year)	Percent conserved	Collector(s)
1936	34	2	1976	6	Archer
1948	58	4	1976	7	Stephens-Hartley
1959	224	87	1963	39	Gregory-Krapovickas-Pietrarelli
1961	61	35	1963	57	Gregory-Krapovickas-Pietrarelli
1964–1967	11	8	1975	73	Gregory-Krapovickas-Pietrarelli
1968	117	65	1975	56	Hammons-Langford-Krapovickas
1976	43	30	1983	70	IBPGR Teams†
1977	96	81	1983	84	IBPGR Teams
1979	7	7	1983	100	IBPGR Teams
1980	37	37	1983	100	IBPGR Teams
1981	54	50	1983	93	IBPGR Teams
1982	64	61	1983	96	IBPGR Teams
1983	52	50	1983	96	IBPGR Teams

† See Appendix I for IBPGR team members.

members). Gregory and Krapovickas were team co-leaders until 1980. Upon Gregory's retirement, Simpson assumed Gregory's responsibilities as team co-leader. In 1980 CENARGEN/EMBRAPA, Brazil, received IBPGR funding for more active participation in *Arachis* exploration and Valls was designated the leader of Brazilian *Arachis* collection.

The 17 expeditions have included (at one time or another) the eight men mentioned above as expedition leader, co-leader, or participant; plus 14 others who were full-time team participants (see Appendix I) on at least one expedition. In addition, no less than 25 "local collaborators" have spent from 1 to 6 days with one or more expeditions. Local contacts have numbered almost 100. The latter included persons who have provided information, further contacts, collection permits and/or useful advice and letters of introduction. In our *Arachis* exploration we have often divided the personnel into two teams: one collecting cultivated materials, the other collecting wild species.

Disposition of Collected Materials. The most important part of planning any collection expedition is the plan for disposition of the materials. A definite commitment needs to be secured from state, national, and/or international centers for receipt and conservation of any materials collected. The problem of initial increase and/or conservation can be illustrated by the example genus, *Arachis*. Table 1 shows the various major collections of wild *Arachis* species from 1936 to 1983. Of the 548 collections made prior to 1976, only 37% of these were conserved until 1975. Since 1976 the record looks better, with 90% conserved. However, the attrition rate increases with each passing year.

ORGANIZATION

General. Organization of an expedition begins by contacting key team members and furnishing an outline of the dates of the proposed collection. Leaders will find it most helpful to solicit suggestions from other team members for persons and institutions to be visited, including contacts for appropriate clearance and permits for doing the work. This process will vary according to the area of collection. In Latin America, it is also essential to keep local police and military authorities informed of your activities. In Semi-Arid Tropical (SAT) Africa contact must be established in accordance with the proper order of protocol. Other areas will have similar requirements.

It is important to compile a list of consulate and consular officers representing the countries of the various team members from countries other than the one in which collection is planned. It is wise to contact these officials and inform them of your plans, providing them with a calendar of proposed arrivals and departures. Each team member should obtain the necessary documents and health certificates required for international travel. A complete battery of inoculations is recommended.

Contact should be established with quarantine personnel, both in the country of collection and in the country where collected materials are to be transported. Preparations must be made to meet quarantine requirements.

As much additional data as possible should be gathered on the proposed collection area. Bennett (4) lists several items of interest including (1) annual rainfall and distribution patterns, (2) planting and harvest season for cultivated crops, (3) available transportation and condition of roads (if they exist), and (4) materials previously collected in the area and their status.

Collection Permits. Early contact should be made in the countries of proposed collection to determine whether or not collection permits are required. Some countries leave these matters to one higher official (e.g., Minister of Agriculture); whereas others require approval by a National Committee on germplasm resources. For peanut collection, it has taken from a few minutes in the office of a Minister of Agriculture to a prolonged process of 27 months to obtain collection permits. As expected, the more highly organized systems of agricultural research require longer periods of time for approval.

Assigning Responsibilities. As the date for the expedition approaches, one should establish a division of labor and responsibility for each team member with designated first assistants who, after discharging their own responsibility, become available to help others. A general rule is to make this organization flexible, and follow the lines of natural interests and capabilities of the several team members. For peanut collections, the divisions have worked well, and the team members have coordinated their capabilities into very efficient collection teams: botanist collecting herbarium specimens, taxonomist recording surrounding vegetation, agronomist recording soil type, collecting nodules, seed, and/or plants, etc.

Collection Forms. Collectors should adopt a specific form for recording collection data. The form format may be partly mandated by the type of funding received and partly by the material to be collected. The USDA has a standard collection form, as does IBPGR. The goal of any form is the same—documentation of collections. If a collection team decides to utilize its own form, strong emphasis should be placed on a format that is computer compatable. Scientists may be able to do this on their own, but if not, a computer consultant should be utilized. Essential data should include: name of sponsor(s) of expedition; country of collection; state, province, city and/or village of collection; collection date; collection number; collector's names; type of collection, i.e., seeds, plants, rhizomes, etc.; latitude, longitude, elevation; surrounding vegetation; local name; grower's name; scientific name, family, genus, species; soil type; topography; and season collected. Additional data might include: stability of environment, amount of erosion, diseases or insects present, stoniness of soil, drainage of site and/or soil.

Disposition of Materials. The final step in organizing the expedition is, as previously stated, the most important and should include a specific plan. Arrangements and definitive plans for the receipt and conservation of the collections in national and/or international centers should be made. For some crops this system is well organized and very efficient. In the case of *Arachis*, we encouraged each team member to take care of this responsibility according to his country's specific requirements. For cultivated peanut, all systems have worked well. For the wild *Arachis* species, difficulties have been encountered. Because of quarantine difficulties we have been unable to utilize ICRISAT, the international center, for initial deposit and multiplication. Brazil, in collaboration with IBPGR, is attempting to establish a live collection of wild *Arachis* species.

With regard to the USA, we have made considerable effort to have a secondary center established by the USDA Plant Introduction System; however, this course of action has not been successful. Personnel and funds for this activity are yet to be secured. In lieu of this appropriate path, we have had no alternative but to assign the responsibility for primary increase and later conservation to those team members willing to take on the work. There is much to be said for the choice of this path. It provides for the people with the most vital interest in the survival of the material the opportunity to have the basic resources at their hands. On the other hand, there are grave faults in this system. First, there is the practical nature of personnel and their basic interests which, with retirements and transfers, expose the germplasm collections to the great danger of neglect or even destruction. There is the more immediate reluctance of local agricultural research administration to permit the expenditure of funds, allocated for other purposes, for germplasm maintenance and distribution; and even greater reluctance to provide additional funds for the specific purpose of maintaining and distributing germplasm. The appropriate route of providing a secondary germplasm center has been sufficiently unpopular so that no such center has been provided which can reproduce, increase, and distribute the wild species of *Arachis*, especially those difficult species which form few or no seeds under conditions in the USA. [For example: in the section *Rhizomatosae nom. nud.*, we must depend on vegetative propagation, greenhouse overwintering, and all the attendant costs and personnel effort. This brings protests from the administrator who has to pay the personnel, the fuel bills, greenhouse construction costs and maintenance and yet in this section *Rhizomatosae* lies almost total immunity to three and possibly more of the most serious pests of the cultivated peanut—leafspot [*Cercospora arachidicola* Hori and *Cercosporidium personatum* (Berk. and Curt.) Deighton], peanut rust (*Puccinia arachidis* Speg), and two-spotted mites (*Tetranychus urticae* Koch). At present these genetic factors cannot be transferred to cultivated peanut, but await the development of the technologies of tissue culture and DNA-plasmid transduction, lying over the scientific horizon, for exploitation in plant breeding.] Without a national center, a temporary substitute procedure for germplasm maintenance is now in operation for the wild peanut species in the USA. A part of this procedure is the well-organized process of national registry of all plant collections by the office of Plant Introduction (PI) of the USDA. After this registration of PI numbers and their entrance into the national catalogue, there is a more or less informal arrangement with members of the research arm of USDA and the state experiment stations for the reproduction and distribution of wild species of *Arachis*. I urge (in accord with the peanut Crops Advisory Committee (CAC) recommendations), in lieu of a secondary center and as a matter of national crop priority, that this system be given substance and continuum by the immediate employment of a curator for peanut at the Plant Introduction Station at Experiment, GA, and the assignment of necessary funds for providing grants to chosen institutions and personnel, in a formally recognized administrative framework in the USDA, to meet the objectives of the National Genetics Resources Board in the case of peanut. A national secondary center for wild *Arachis* germplasm could then be formed within the proposed and present framework with the sole functions of coordination, receiving, cold storage, and distribution.

IMPLEMENTATION

General. If proper planning and organization have been done, the matter of implementation will be routine—as much so as exploration expeditions can be. Alternate plans should always be available because unforeseen weather, changes in governments, public elections, religious holidays, and illness of team members can turn the best made plans to shambles in short order.

In executing a plant exploration plan, team members must remember that patience must reign supreme, or frustration will become dominant. The freedom of "doing things my way," does not always exist. A planned objective may be reached, but by what one may consider a very circuitous route. One must remember that local law and custom should be followed, always mindful that the local people's pride and dignity are probably just as strong as your own.

Arachis. The 17 expeditions to collect *Arachis* were initiated in December 1976. The areas covered from 1976 to 1983 are shown in Fig. 2. Collections were made in Argentina, Bolivia, Brazil, Ecuador, Paraguay, and Peru.

Table 2 indicates the year, expedition number, teams, and number of collections of cultivated and wild species of *Arachis*, 1976 to 1983.

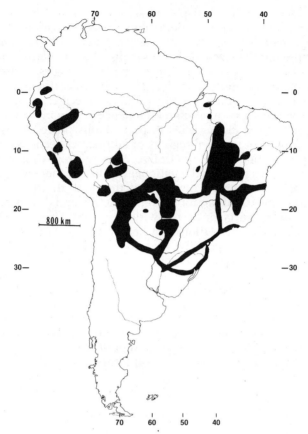

Fig. 2. Areas of *Arachis* germplasm exploration 1976 to 1983.

Our travel was accomplished by commercial aircraft, air taxi, bus, passenger train, freight train, car, truck, jeep, motorcycle, river boat, river barge, motorboat, dugout canoe, cable car, ox cart, and a lot of walking. We often had to change our plans concerning the mode of transport to fit local conditions after our arrival.

The team carried essential collection gear and as much additional equipment as possible. For the herbarium a small portable dryer, plant presses, newspapers for folders, and plastic bags were included. Materials for live plant collection included plastic bags, labels, and sphagnum moss. In order to make seed collections the team carried labels, paper bags, and envelopes, and cloth bags of several sizes. When possible the team carried various tools for digging and a small sifting screen. Nodules were collected in 7.5 mL, screw top plastic vials with a drying agent and cotton plug inside. More thorough lists of needed supplies have been presented by Bennett (4) and Hawkes (17). For our conditions, much of what was listed there would have been impossible to include for reasons listed under team selection.

Sampling of populations has been discussed by Allard (1), Bennett (4), and Marshall and Brown (22). Our collection of *Arachis* has been

Table 2. *Arachis* materials collected in South America, 1976 to 1983.

Expedition			Number Arachis sp	Number Arachis hypogaea	Number probable new species
Year	No.	Team(s)†			
1976	1	1	43	0	6
1977	2	2, 3, 4, 5	46	125	4
1977	3	6, 7, 8	50	8	
1978	4	19	(45)‡	5	(5)‡
1979	5	9, 10	7	25	1
1980	6 I	11, 12, 13, 14, 15	37	102	3
1980	6 II	16, 17	0	27	
1981	7	21	2	10	1
1981	8	18	0	67	
1981	9	20, 22	9	40	6
1981	10	23	43	9	3
1981	11	24	0	40	
1982	12	25	44	6	3
1982	13	26	20	12	2
1983	14	27	30	1	
1983	15	15, 28	7	138	
1983	16	29	15	15	
1983	17	4	0	54	
			353	684	29

† See Appendix I for team member identification.
‡ Not new collections, but new introductions to the USA.

done with the basics of sampling in mind, but, as stated by Bennett (4), "Samples cannot be more representative than conditions in the field permit, and these may often be severely limiting." Our basic sample size for cultivated peanut in a market has been 1 kg (750 to 4000 seeds). However, if we encountered a small-scale farmer who only had 1 kg to plant his entire crop, we have often been satisfied to collect 20 to 30 seeds. For the wild *Arachis* we have strived to make our samples representative of the population being collected. Size of colonies has varied from one plant to vast populations covering several hectare. Time has often been our limiting factor in the large populations; rarely have we had the luxury of more than 3 h at one site, and usually much less.

As the wild *Arachis* species collections were made, herbarium specimens and nodule samples were taken. The dried specimens were deposited at Corrientes, Argentina, or Brazilia, Brazil, and will be duly distributed to appropriate world herbaria. The nodule collections were deposited at North Carolina State University for isolation and distribution to ICRISAT.

Wild species collections were made as seeds, if at all possible. Only when no seed could be found were live plants collected. At most sites, soil type, elevation, latitude, longitude, surrounding vegetation, and other data were recorded.

Arachis Materials. The cultivated peanut materials collected on these expeditions included all four botanical varieties (10) of the cultivated species. Most of the material collected in Bolivia was what Gregory et al. (10) referred to as "Bolivian" and belonged to the virginia (var. *hypogaea*) type. The Peruvian collections correspond to the "Peruvian" (10) or valencia type (*A. hypogaea fastigiata* var. *fastigiata*). The materials from Paraguay were valencia and spanish (var. *vulgaris*). Cultivated collections from Brazil were quite varied and included spanish, valencia, and virginia types. The latter included some types that appeared intermediate between the Bolivian and the type identified as *A. nambyquarae*. Only two or three *A. hypogaea* var. *hirsuta* types were found in Peru.

The wild species collections included materials representing the seven sections identified by Gregory et al. (10, 11) and Gregory and Gregory (9). The diversity of these collections will be shown by future descriptions of at least 29 new species not included in collections prior to 1976.

Two hundred and eighty-eight nodule collections were made from wild and cultivated peanut and other legumes.

Information. In addition to collecting germplasm, the *Arachis* teams have gained valuable information which has been useful in further collection and will be beneficial for collection of additional materials in the future. The sources of new information ranged from small bits of herbarium specimens found in various herbaria which were collected by explorers of the 18th and 19th centuries, to information from a tribal chief in the jungle of North Bolivia. "Word-of-mouth" information may prove to be misleading or erroneous, but it has usually been reliable and has often lead to collection of a landrace or a wild species not previously included in germplasm collections.

Distribution of the Sections. The expeditions have greatly extended the known distribution of the sections of genus *Arachis*. There was a good measure of this fact because Gregory et al. (10) had outlined the areas of known distribution just prior to these expeditions. Figures 3 to 6 show the distributions of the sections before 1976 and as of June 1983.

Section *Arachis nom. nud.* ($2n = 20$ and $2n = 4x = 40$) (Fig. 3), to which the cultivated peanut belongs, was extended 1000 km northwest into the North Beni of Bolivia, approximately 1500 km northeast into the lower Tocantins river valley of Brazil (see Fig. 7 for locations of rivers) and about 350 km further north on the Atlantic coast. Additionally, at least 10 new species of section *Arachis* were collected within the previously known distribution of the section.

Section *Triseminalae nom. nud.* ($2n = 20$) (Fig. 3) was collected in an area along the Rio Sao Francisco which more than doubled the known area of distribution.

The area of known distribution of section *Ambinervosae nom. nud.* ($2n = 20$) was more than doubled (Fig. 4), now extending much farther south and west in Northeast Brazil.

Several collections of section *Erectoidae nom. nud.* ($2n = 20$) were made, but only one affected the known area of distribution (Fig. 4), extending the section almost 200 km farther east.

The known distribution of section *Extranervosae nom. nud.* ($2n = 20$) (Fig. 5) was almost tripled in size, now extending much farther north and east in Northeast Brazil.

Recent studies (unpublished data) have indicated that series *Procumbensae nom. nud.* (10) should be elevated to section *Procumbensae nom.*

nud. ($2n$ = 20). The area of known distribution (Fig. 5) of these species was more than doubled by connecting the two previous areas of collection in Southwest Brazil and Central Bolivia.

The known area of section *Caulorhizae nom. nud.* ($2n$ = 20) (Fig. 6) was almost tripled with collections from the western Rio Jequitinhonha, the upper Sao Francisco valley, and farther west into the upper regions of the Tocantins valley.

Section *Rhizomatosae nom. nud.* series *Eurhizomatosae nom. nud.* ($2n$ = $4x$ = 40) (Fig. 6) was not extended very much, but series *Prorhizomatosae nom. nud.* ($2n$ = 20) (Fig. 6) was extended east to the Atlantic Coast.

Importance of Arachis Collections. Significant aspects of the collections of *Arachis* relate to the 15, or more, new species which belong to section *Arachis*. All of these will probably cross directly with *A. hypogaea* and can be direct sources of genetic characteristics. These collections will contribute significantly to the improvement of the cultivated peanut in the future if they can be conserved. It is important to note that section *Arachis* was collected much farther north (Fig. 3) than before. What appear to be annual species of section *Arachis* can survive in forested swamp land, and this indicates genetic variability may be broader than previously imagined. This variability will likely present some breeding problems, but will undoubtedly provide valuable genetic characters. The northern collections suggest that an additional 800 000 km^2 of Amazon drainage need to be explored for *Arachis* wild species. This region would include the area of Brazil bounded by the Amazon on the north, Rio Madeira and Rio Guapore on the west, the southern rim of the Amazon drainage on the south, and the Tocantins valley on the east (Fig. 7).

The collections made from 1976 to 1983 and related information indicate that the peanut is cultivated in almost all regions of tropical and temperate South America (to 35°S), up to an elevation near 2000 m, and from near desert to tropical rain forest. Many landraces exist, but these are being lost with increasing frequency as agriculture rapidly develops. Brazil and Argentina are foremost in loss frequency.

Phylogenetic studies of the collections may help clarify the evolution of the *Arachis* genus. For example, we have found, in addition to the previously known sympatric sections *Rhizomatosae—Erectoidae* and *Rhizomatosae—Extranervosae—Arachis*, that several more sections overlap in their distributions: sections *Ambinervosae* and *Caulorhizae* overlap; sections *Caulorhizae* and *Triseminalae* overlap; and section *Extranervosae* overlaps with both *Caulorhizae* and *Triseminalae*. Prior to 1976 (10), none of these section overlaps were known to occur. In some cases, species from different sections were found growing sympatrically. This shows that the sections are not as geographically isolated as previously supposed, and that genetic isolation is strong, since the sections can grow sympatrically and maintain the integrity of each. It also may indicate that evolutionary processes are still at work.

The wild *Arachis* species continue to survive in many areas, and perhaps are actually favored by clearing of the "cerrado" for grazing. However, when an area is put to cultivation by modern farm equipment, the wild species are lost in short order. Again, Argentina's and Brazil's rapid

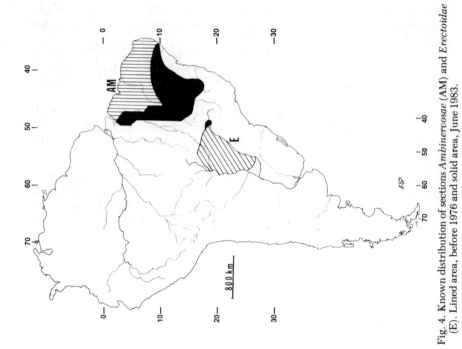

Fig. 4. Known distribution of sections *Ambinervosae* (AM) and *Erectoidae* (E). Lined area, before 1976 and solid area, June 1983.

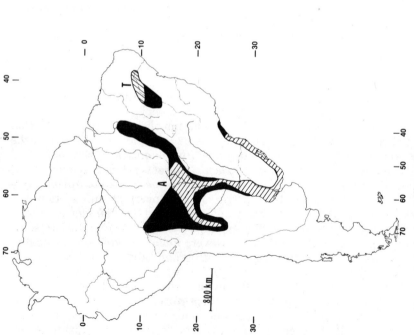

Fig. 3. Known distribution of sections *Arachis* (A) and *Triseminalae* (T). Lined area, before 1976 and solid area, June 1983.

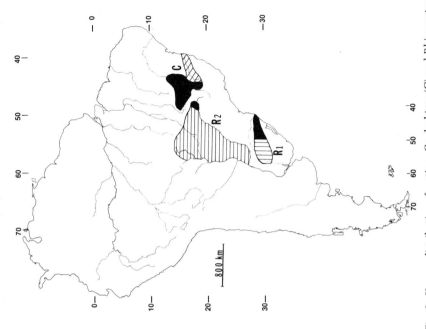

Fig. 6. Known distribution of sections *Caulorhizae* (C) and *Rhizomatosae* (R₁ = *Prorhizomatosae*, R₂ = *Eurhizomatosae*). Lined area, before 1976 and solid area, June 1983.

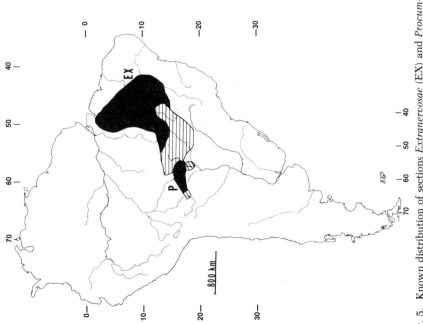

Fig. 5. Known distribution of sections *Extranervosae* (EX) and *Procumbensae* (P). Lined area, before 1976 and solid area, June 1983.

Fig. 7. Major rivers of South America.

advancement of technology and machinery will continue to cause rapid losses in the wild *Arachis* species. Eastern Bolivia, however, will continue to be a haven for valuable *Arachis* species. To date no wild *Arachis* species have been collected from Peru.

From our observations, it is obvious that collection of wild and cultivated germplasm of peanut needs to be completed in Argentina and Brazil very soon. The IBPGR project of these expeditions and another project involving IBPGR, CENARGEN (Brazil), and ICRISAT are designed to do this work as rapidly as possible. Future collections must be centered in Brazil, Bolivia, Paraguay, and Uruguay. Landraces of *A. hypogaea* most surely exist in other countries of South America, as well as Central America, and should be considered the object of future collection expeditions.

CONCLUSION

In my concluding statements, I want to reiterate the problem of conservation and to leave one thought foremost in the reader's mind. Germplasm which is collected must be preserved for utilization. There is an acknowledged need to direct funds to the support of combined research in tissue culture and DNA technology. In doing this, a process which is already in progress, the temptation to overemphasize the novel at the expense of the usual must be resisted so as to achieve a program balance. These new areas of work in biotechnology definitely need to be pursued because of their potential. However, caution should be exercised so that funds are not siphoned from germplasm exploration and conservation. Genetic transfers have only been accomplished in a few species which are noted for their responsiveness. These efforts are some distance from being able to fabricate DNA sequences to produce even one useful plant gene. This means that even if transfers of specific sequences of DNA become commonplace in all plant species, the source of desired sequences for the improvement of a cultigen will remain, for a long time to come, the species relatives of the cultigen under improvement. Consequently, the persons and organizations who may seem to be supplanting the need for natural genetic resources will be the very ones who stand to gain the most from a well conceived and properly conducted program of germplasm conservation. It will do no good to provide resources for the biochemist to learn how to make DNA transfers and then deny them the germplasm from which to obtain the sequences. This would indeed be shortsighted and fruitless.

ACKNOWLEDGMENTS

The author wishes to acknowledge the effort of all the persons and agencies who have supported the *Arachis* explorations, especially the IBPGR and CENARGEN. A special thanks goes to Drs. W. C. Gregory and M. P. Gregory for their part in the preparation of this manuscript. Sincere appreciation is expressed to Mrs. V. June Wetwiska for her skills and patience in completion of this manuscript.

APPENDIX
ARACHIS COLLECTION 1976–1983. TEAM MEMBERS, SUPPORTING AGENCY, AND COLLECTION TEAMS.

Team Members and Their Supporting Agencies

Team Leaders and/or Co-leaders

D. J. Banks, (B)†, U.S. Department of Agricuture and Oklahoma State University, Stillwater, OK.

W. C. Gregory, (G), North Carolina State University and North Carolina Agricultural Experiment Station, Raleigh, NC.

A. Krapovickas, (K), Universidad Nacional del Nordeste, Corrientes, Argentina.

J. Pietrarelli, (P), Instituto Nacional de Tecnologia Agropecuaria (INTA) and Manfredi Estacion Experimental Agropecuaria, Manfredi, Argentina.

A. Schinini, (Sc), Universidad Nacional del Nordeste, Corrientes, Argentina.

———————————— *Appendix continued* ————————————

Team Leaders and/or Co-leaders

C. E. Simpson (S), Texas Agricultural Experiment Station and Texas A&M University, Stephenville, TX.

J. F. M. Valls, (V), Centro Nacional de Recursos Geneticos (CENARGEN) EMBRAPA, Brazilia, Brazil.

H. Zurita O., (Z), Centro de Investigacion Agricola Tropical (CIAT) and Saavedra Estacion Experimental, Santa Cruz, Bolivia.

Team Participants

V. O. Arriola, (A), Instituto Nacional de Investigacion Agraria (INIA), Cuzco, Peru.

L. Coradin, (C), CENARGEN/EMBRAPA, Brazilia, Brazil.

M. Corro R., (Co), Universidad Juan Misael Saracho, Tarija, Bolivia.

M. A. N. Gerin, (Ge), Instituto Agronomico, Campinas, Sao Paulo, Brazil.

R. W. Gibbons, (Gb), International Crops Research Institute for the Semi-Arid Tropics, Patancheru, A.P., India.

A. Gripp, (Gr), CENARGEN/EMBRAPA, Brazilia, Brazil.

L. Janicki, (J), PRODES, LaPaz, Bolivia.

A. R. Miranda, (M), CENARGEN/EMBRAPA, Brazilia, Brazil.

J. P. Moss, (Mo), Cytogeneticist, ICRISAT, Patancheru, A.P., India.

V. R. Rao, (R), Genetic Resources Unit, ICRISAT, Patancheru, A.P., India.

G. P. Silva, (Sv), CENARGEN/EMBRAPA, Brazilia, Brazil.

R. F. de Arruda Veiga, (Ve), Instituto Agronomico, Campinas, Sao Paulo, Brazil.

W. L. Werneck, (W), CENARGEN/EMBRAPA, Brazilia, Brazil.

R. H. Zanini, (Zi), INTA, Manfredi Estacion Experimental Agropecuaria, Manfredi, Argentina.

Collection Teams

1.‡GK†	8. Sc	15. KSSc	22. C
2. GKBSPSc	9. GKSPScGb	16. SP	23. VSGr
3. GKBSPScZ	10. GKSPSc	17. SPA	24. PZi
4. BPZ	11. SB	18. SPZ	25. VKR
5. GKSSc	12. KSBScC	19. S	26. VSW
6. GKPSc	13. BZC	20. VMSv	27. VKSvVe
7. KSc	14. BZCJ	21. V	28. KSScCo
			29. VSMoSvGe

† Abbreviation for team member(s).
‡ Designates team number.

REFERENCES

1. Allard, R. W. 1970. Population structure and sampling methods. p. 97–107. *In* O. H. Frankel and E. Bennett (ed.) Genetic resources in plants—Their exploration and conservation. IBP Handb. no. 11. London. Blackwell Scientific Publications, Oxford.

2. ――――. 1960. Principles of plant breeding. John Wiley & Sons, New York.

3. Banks, D. J. 1976. Peanuts: Germplasm resources. Crop Sci. 16:499–502.

4. Bennett, E. 1970. Tactics of plant exploration. p. 157–180. *In* O. H. Frankel and E. Bennett (ed.) Genetic resources in plants—Their exploration and conservation. IBP Handb. no. 11. London. Blackwell Scientific Publications, Oxford.

5. Briggs, F. N., and P. F. Knowles. 1967. Introduction to plant breeding. Reinhold Publishing Corp., New York.

6. Chang, T. T. (ed.) 1972. Rice breeding. International Rice Research Institute. Los Baños, Philippines.

7. ――――, S. D. Sharma, C. R. Adair, and A. T. Perez. 1972. Manual for field collectors of rice. International Rice Research Institute. Los Baños, Philippines.

8. Frankel, O. H., and E. Bennett (ed.) 1970. Genetic resources in plants—Their exploration and conservation. IBP Handb. no. 11. London. Blackwell Scientific Publications, Oxford.

9. Gregory, M. P., and W. C. Gregory. 1979. Exotic germ plasm of *Arachis* L. interspecific hybrids. J. Hered. 70:185–193.

10. Gregory, W. C., M. P. Gregory, A. Krapovickas, B. W. Smith, and J. A. Yarbrough. 1973. Structure and genetic resources of peanuts. p. 47–134. *In* C. T. Wilson (ed.) Peanut culture and uses. Am. Peanut Res. and Educ. Assoc., Stillwater, OK.

11. ――――, A. Krapovickas, and M. P. Gregory. 1980. Structure, variation, evolution, and classification in *Arachis*. *In* K. P. Summerfield and B. R. Bunting (ed.) Advances in legume science. Kew, London.

12. Gregory, W. C. 1976–1983. Personal communication.

13. Hammons, R. O. 1976. Peanuts: Germplasm resources. Crop Sci. 16:527–530.

14. Harlan, J. R. 1956. Distribution and utilization of natural variability in cultivated plants. Brookhaven Symposia in Biology 9:191–208.

15. ――――. 1976. Genetic resources in wild relatives of crops. Crop Sci. 16:329–333.

16. Hawkes, J. G. 1976. Manual for field collectors (Seed Crops). AGPE: Misc./7. FAO, Rome.

17. ――――. 1980. Crop genetic resources field collection manual. IBPGR-EUCARPIA. Univ. of Birmingham, Birmingham.

18. International Rice Research Institute. 1978. Proc. of the workshop on the genetic conservation of rice. International Rice Research Institute-International Board for Plant Genetic Resources. Los Baños, Philippines.

19. Krapovickas, A. 1977–1983. Personal communication.

20. ――――. 1973. Evolution of the genus *Arachis*. *In* Rom Moau (ed.) Agricultural genetics—Selected topics. John Wiley & Sons, New York.

21. ――――. 1968. Origin, variabilidad y difusion del mani (*Arachis hypogaea*). Actas y Memorias XXXVII Congreso Internacional Americanistas 2—517–553. English translation in: p. 427–441. P. J. Ucko and G. W. Dimbleby (ed.) 1969. The domestication and exploitation of plants and animals. Duckworth, London.

22. Marshall, D. R., and A. H. D. Brown. 1975. Optimum sampling strategies in genetic conservation. p. 53–80. *In* O. H. Frankel and J. G. Hawkes (ed.) Crop genetic resources for today and tomorrow. Cambridge University Press, New York.

23. Stelly, M. (ed.) 1975. Agronomy Abstracts—1975 Annual Meetings, ASA, CSSA, SSSA. Knoxville, Tenn.

24. Varnell, R. J., and D. E. McCloud (ed.) 1975. Germplasm preservation and genotype evaluation in *Arachis* (peanuts). Workshop Report. 11–15 July. Gainesville, FL.

25. Webster, O. J. 1976. Sorghum vulnerability and germplasm resources. Crop Sci. 16: 553–556.

26. Williams, J. T. (exec. sect.) 1980. Annual Report. IBPGR. FAO. Rome, Italy.

27. ————. (exec. sect.) 1981. Annual Report. IBPGR, FAO. Rome, Italy.

28. Wynne, J. C., and W. C. Gregory. 1981. Peanut breeding. Adv. Agron. 34:39–72.

Chapter 2

The International Germplasm Program of the International Board for Plant Genetics Resources[1]

J. T. WILLIAMS[2]

When the International Board for Plant Genetic Resources (IBPGR) was created by the Consultative Group on International Agricultural Research (CGIAR) in 1974 it faced a daunting task. It was given a mandate to develop a world network of plant genetic resources activities into which would be articulated all on-going programs. But, there were few properly organized programs; the priorities were only defined in the broadest terms and the sheer volume of work to be done in a limited time was intimidating.

The Board set about its task, in close association with Food and Agriculture Organization (FAO), by first, identifying crop and geographical priorities (IBPGR, 1976; IBPGR, 1981) and second, initiating field collection for major staple food crops, especially in case of emergency situations. This initial approach was logical in the time frame available to salvage diversity.

Several points become apparent:

1. When the Board took action, this had a remarkable catalytic effect on other organizations. Nowhere was this seen more than with the International Agricultural Research Centers (IARC) of the CGIAR. The Board and the IARCs established joint advisory committees for their mandated crops.

[1] Contribution from the International Board for Plant Genetic Resources.
[2] Executive Secretary, International Board for Plant Genetic Resources.

Copyright © 1984 Crop Science Society of America, 677 South Segoe Road, Madison, WI 53711. *Conservation of Crop Germplasm—An International Perspective.*

2. In order to be effective the Board had to rely on good scientific advice. This was mobilized through committees and working groups; the programs therefore had a sound basis with the voluntary cooperation of hundreds of scientists around the world, knowledgeable on crop genetic resources.

3. By 1978, there was only a handful of genebanks in the world with suitable facilities and equipment to store germplasm (Ng and Williams, 1978). Conservation had to be carried out and the Board began the task of encouraging and assisting countries in the construction of genebanks to handle the major crops. There are now 38 base collections in 20 countries which constitute a designated world network.

4. One problem was that we did not know what was in existing collections. Information was lacking—and still is to a large degree see (Croston and Williams, 1981 for the situation with wheat, *Triticum* spp. L.). This is especially important in cases when genetic diversity in collections is increasing yet limited use is actually being made of the materials. However, breeders are becoming more and more aware of the potential value of the collections and will therefore wish to evaluate materials.

ACCOMPLISHMENTS TO DATE

In this chapter, I shall only summarize the accomplishments to date. Further details can be found in Annual Reports (e.g., IBPGR, 1983) and a review has been provided by Wilkes (1983). On the basis of goodwill, the Board has developed a cooperative network of research centers and agricultural scientists in about 100 countries. As a result of its acting as a catalyst and its initiation of programs, new national genetic resources committees and/or coordinators have been established in about 20 countries and there is active exchange of views between breeders' organizations such as Eucarpia and Sabrao, and coordinated programs in the larger countries such as Brazil, India, USA, and USSR. Many governments have appointed liaison officers specifically to maintain links with IBPGR.

Collecting. Over a period of 9 years the IBPGR has organized and carried out or associated itself with 250 collecting missions in more than 70 countries. Although most missions were for seed crops, action after 1980 was initiated on clonal material, such as sweet potato (*Ipomea batatas*), cassava (*Manihot esculenta*), citrus (*Citrus* spp.), cocoa (*Cacao theobroma*), and others [work by the IBPGR on potato has been minor because the International Potato Center (CIP) had already gathered the material].

Through those missions the maize of Latin America was in part recollected; collection of land races of wheat was largely finished, about half the necessary work was completed for rice (*Oryza* spp.), sorghum (*Sorghum* spp.), pearl millet (*Pennisetum* spp.), groundnut (*Arachis* spp.), okra (*Abelmoschus esculentus*), and tomato (*Lycopersicon esculen-*

tum). Much remains to be done for another 40-odd species and even when most of the areas have been covered there will always be the need for "hot-spot" collection.

Conservation. The IBPGR has provided basic equipment for national genebanks in 20 developing countries and support to develop collections of vegetatively propagated crops. About half of the gene banks supported were for long-term conservation and these have been incorporated into a designated network of base collections. At present, there are 39 centers in 29 countries designated as base collections and they cover 30 seed crops. This network will be complete for all major crops by 1985 to 1986 and increasing attention will be given to the designation of active collections which will have medium-term storage and which carry out evaluation and exchange. A review is provided by Plucknett et al. (1983).

Information. Since many existing collections have not been documented, we have published directories of collections for most major crops, summarizing what is held where. We have accelerated the work on characterization and evaluation by giving financial support, and this will be increased in view of the great need for data. It will be based on standard international descriptor lists compatible with, or at least convertible into, those major national programs; e.g., the USA, the Comecon countries of eastern Europe; and organizations involved with varietal descriptions. By the end of 1983 about 50 lists will be available.

In addition, help has been given to developing countries to allow computerized information retrieval systems to be implemented. About 25 countries have been helped in this way. Also in view of the great importance of the U.S. National Plant Germplasm Information System, a liaison office has been opened at the Agricultural Research Service (ARS), Beltsville, MD.

Cooperation at the Regional Level. Although the Board largely focuses its attention on crops, it is sensitive to the needs of developing countries. It convenes regional intergovernmental consultative meetings, and by the end of this year it will have covered 12 of its 14 priority regions in this way. At the wishes of the countries, regional activities are organized and regional staff are appointed in important parts of the world. They are currently located in Southeast Asia, East Africa, West Africa, and Latin America; some reorganization of support to Southwest Asia, the Mediterranean and South Asia is under way.

One paradox of work at the regional level is that many minor species assume importance at that level, and the Board with its small budget and staff has to limit its support to such crops. Nevertheless, when they are of overriding importance, e.g., the local roots and tubers of the Andes or certain fruits in Southeast Asia, some support is provided.

Research. Although most of what I have outlined is operational, much of the follow-up work by its nature generates research findings. It leads to a clearer understanding of species relationships, the origin and evolution of crops, and patterns of variation. The work is too diverse to outline but the following examples show the range. Work on collection of

Arachis germplasm in Latin America is leading to the understanding of hitherto unknown species; similarly work on eggplants (*Solanum aethiopicum* and other indigenous species) in Africa will provide, for the first time, knowledge of the variability of local species. A major emphasis on collecting *Aegilops* will provide materials for a fuller understanding of the genus and its relationship to wheat. There are dozens of other examples which could be quoted.

Then there is basic research necessary for understanding conservation. The Board has supported research on seed physiology for some years, so that a special manual can be produced for gene bank curators. Even more recently has been the assessment of the state of in vitro culture and cryopreservation. These new methods of germplasm conservation, based on the totipotency of cultures, will have major impact on the preservation of clonal crops so important in the tropics and for crops such as temperate fruits and *Allium*.

In addition some work, although not enough, has been initiated on the handling of outbreeding materials which pose major problems for the maintenance of genetic integrity in collections.

Training. To bridge gaps the Board has supported training to M.S. level of many scientists for the Third World and supports a specifically designed international training course in genetic conservation at the Univ. of Birmingham in the United Kingdom. In addition, over 450 trainees have attended short technical courses in many parts of the world. Recently, an intern scheme at the pre- and postdoctoral level has been initiated. In a few years this should have a major impact on the world network.

NEW DEVELOPMENTS

The present activities have to continue into the foreseeable future so that there will be representative seed samples of all important crops stored in base collections and certain clonal crops established in repositories. Evaluation and data dissemination will have to assume greater significance. These studies will also include forages worldwide and much more emphasis on wild species (e.g., IBPGR/IRRI, 1982).

In order to look to the next 10 years, the Board has started a planning exercise to culminate in a report at the Board's 10th Anniversary in 1984. Although all the details of this are not yet public, two factors are likely to assume significance. First, there are clear scientific reasons for much more detailed ecogeographic survey (using multidisciplinary teams) prior to actual collection. Second, the Board has to keep abreast of developments in the area of genetic manipulation because such developments will render the germplasm collections even more valuable as sources of genes. Documentation will have to be accelerated in some cases even to the point of using gene symbols.

With the budget running currently at about $4 million per year, we are unlikely to be able to expand to cover minor species, nor indeed to fund more than a small part of the total. In fact in 1982 the CGIAR's input globally was 25% of all inputs worldwide and the IBPGR's input was small, but generated worldwide interest and some significant results (CGIAR, 1982). The Board intends to vigorously pursue the leadership role entrusted to it.

Lastly, there has been a great deal of controversy and publicity about germplasm in recent years (largely from a lay audience which is more concerned with the impact of multinational companies and variety rights). Many reports have been naive and lack a technical background in genetic resources. They have, however, attracted more public attention than we could have developed to raise the awareness for action. A balanced review has been provided by Brown (1983). The FAO is also considering mechanisms whereby an international network could in fact guarantee the availability of materials and information.

REFERENCES

1. Brown, W. L. 1983. Genetic diversity and genetic vulnerability—An appraisal. Econ. Bot. 37:4–12.

2. Consultative Group on International Agricultural Research. 1982. Integrative report, Washington, DC.

3. Croston, R., and J. T. Williams. 1981. A world survey of wheat genetic resources. International Board for Plant Genetic Resources, Rome, Italy.

4. International Board for Plant Genetic Resources. 1976. Priorities among crops and regions. Rome, Italy.

5. ----. 1981. Revised priorities among crops and regions. Rome, Italy.

6. ----. 1983. Annual report 1982. Rome, Italy.

7. ----, and International Rice Research Institute. Rice Advisory Committee. 1982. Conservation of the wild rices of tropical Asia. Plant Genet. Resour. Newsl. 49:13–18.

8. Ng, Q., and J. T. Williams. 1978. Seed stores for crop genetic conservation. Food and Agriculture Organization/International Board for Plant Genetic Resources, Rome, Italy.

9. Plucknett, D. L., N. J. A. Smith, J. T. Williams, and N. M. Anishetty. 1983. Crop germplasm conservation and developing countries. Science 220:163–169.

10. Van Sloten, D. H., and C. J. Bishop. 1982. The IBPGR program for the conservation of horticultural genetic resources. 21st Int. Hortic. Congr., Hamburg. September 1982.

11. Wilkes, G. 1983. Current status of crop plant germplasm. CRC Review. Plant Sci. 1: 133–181.

Chapter 3

A National Plant Germplasm System

QUENTIN JONES[1]

The USA, which stands unchallenged as the greatest producer of food that the world has ever known and which exports the production from 1 acre in 3, is dependent upon the rest of the world for its genetic resources (germplasm) of practically all of its crop plants. That is why plant introduction activities started long before the first European colonists arrived. Archeological plant materials from Bat Cave, NM (Smith, 1950), document a cultural series from about 2500 B.C. to about A.D. 1000. Plant remains included corn (*Zea mays* L.), pumpkin (*Curcurbita pepo* L.), and beans (*Phaseolus* spp.). None showed the range of diversity over time that has been found in caves in Mexico and elsewhere further Fouth. Plant introduction by American Indians or Amerinds had been going on for more than 3000 years prior to the arrival of the pilgrims.

Plant introduction was formalized by the Federal Government as early as 1827, when American consuls abroad were directed by President John Quincy Adams to acquire crop seeds and dispatch them to the USA (Hodge and Erlanson, 1955). Plant introduction and distribution formed the central core of the U.S. Department of Agriculture (USDA) when the latter was founded in 1862. The new Department was to "acquire and diffuse. . .useful information on subjects connected with agriculture in the most general and comprehensive sense of that word, and to *procure*, propagate, and distribute among the people new and valuable seeds and plants" (Ross, 1946).

Following creation of the USDA, plant exploration activities increased. Collectors were sent to Europe and China in 1864, to the latter for Chinese sorghums (*Sorghum bicolor* L. Moench). Efforts up to 1898

[1] National Program Staff, USDA-ARS, BARC-West, Beltsville, MD 20705.

Copyright © 1984 Crop Science Society of America, 677 South Segoe Road, Madison, WI 53711. *Conservation of Crop Germplasm—An International Perspective.*

brought introductions of the navel orange [*Citrus sinensis* L. (Osb.)], flax (*Linum usitatissimum* L.), olive (*Olea enropaca* L.), persimmon (*Diospyros kako* L.), sorghum, wheats (*Triticum* spp.), and other cereals. Many introductions of temperate fruits and vegetables were brought in from Europe. Finally, by 1898, the USDA's activities and interests in the introduction of new plants had become so great that a new unit, the Section of Seed and Plant Introduction, was established. With a modest beginning and an allotment of $2000, a foundation was laid for an increasing level of activity that has had a profound effect on American agriculture.

PLANT INTRODUCTIONS (1898–1983)

Since 1898, over 400 000 plant introductions have reached the hands of American scientists and those of scientists in many other countries. More than 200 actual foreign explorations to centers of crop diversity have been undertaken. But numbers alone do not tell the story. Two years after the Section of Seed and Plant Introduction was created, the rediscovery of Mendel's laws of inheritance triggered the development of plant breeding as a science. This in turn gradually, but dramatically, changed plant introduction objectives from transplanting crops from other parts of the world into U.S. agriculture to supplying sources of genes to meet crop breeding objectives.

The next very important milestone was the passing of the Research and Marketing Act (Public Law-733) by the 80th Congress in 1946. This Act authorized funds to the States for cooperative research in which two or more State agricultural experiment stations cooperated to meet common objectives. This "regional research fund" was to be used only for cooperative regional projects recommended by a committee of nine persons, elected by and representing, the directors of the State agricultural experiment stations, and approved by the Secretary of Agriculture. The same Act also authorized the appropriation of funds for use by the USDA for cooperative research with the State agricultural experiment stations.

As a result of this Act, the four Regional Plant Introduction Stations (Geneva, NY; Experiment, GA; Ames, IA; and Pullman, WA), the Interregional Potato Project (IR-1), and the National Seed Storage Laboratory were planned and implemented over the next 10 years as funds became available.

Throughout the 1960s, budgets for plant germplasm remained level, while the purchasing power of those budgets decreased. Then in 1970, the southern corn leaf blight (*Helminthorposium maydis*) epidemic struck. Our corn crop was vulnerable to southern corn leaf blight because, among other reasons, a single source of cytoplasm had been utilized in developing a major portion of the corn hybrids. There suddenly appeared a new strain of the fungus pathogen well adapted to that so-called Texas cytoplasm, and favorable weather conditions promoted its sweep over the corn crop. Corn yield dropped an estimated 50% or more in some Southern States and 15% nationwide.

Thanks to good corn weather the following year and to heroic efforts by seedsmen, scientists, and farmers, the epidemic that year was mild. The scientific and public reaction to the corn blight epidemic was not so mild. There was widespread concern that such a disaster could happen in this, the world's leading country in agriculture and agricultural science. The National Academy of Sciences responded to this concern and set up a Committee on Genetic Vulnerability of Major Crops to find answers to the questions, "How uniform genetically are other crops upon which the nation depends, and how vulnerable, therefore, are they to epidemics?" The Committee's answer was that most major crops are impressively uniform genetically and impressively vulnerable (Committee on Genetic Vulnerability of Major Crops, 1972). The Committee's report was published in 1972 and crystallized a long-standing concern among germplasm biologists that the rescue, preservation, and use of genetic diversity of the world's crop plants and their wild relatives were being sadly neglected and rapidly eroded.

Since 1972, there has been a worldwide awakening to the fact that genetic resources, plant and animal, are of at least equal importance to the three—soil, water, air—traditionally accepted as our "natural resources." In 1974, the International Board for Plant Genetic Resources (IBPGR) was established by the Consultative Group on International Agricultural Research (CGIAR). In the same year, the U.S. National Plant Germplasm Committee (NPGC) was established and began conceptualizing and organizing a national effort involving the USDA, the State agricultural experiment stations, and commercial interests involved in crop improvement and the seed trade. In 1975, the Secretary of Agriculture appointed the National Plant Genetic Resources Board (NPGRB). The NPGRB was a direct outgrowth of the alarm caused by the southern corn leaf blight.

So we now have a National Plant Germplasm System (NPGS) that provides access to over 400 000 accessions of seed and clonal germplasm (Jones and Gillette, 1982). This system represents a good start on acquiring and preserving the genetic diversity of economic plants and their wild relatives. The NPGS is pursuing and accelerating programs to acquire, maintain, and evaluate for use as wide as possible a range of genetic diversity of these plants before it is lost forever because of man's adverse impacts on natural environments and changes being made in agricultural patterns and practices.

Plant germplasm has caught the attention of agricultural administrators and national legislators. Now we need to take full advantage of better budgets and do the best possible job as stewards of this irreplaceable resource.

What are we doing now to improve our stewardship of plant germplasm? A summary by program function follows.

ACQUISITION—(EXPLORATION, COLLECTION)

Our germplasm collecting expeditions since World War II have been largely centered on specific needs for material having resistance to biological or physical stresses. It was generally felt that we were filling "gaps" in collections already in gene banks. Sometimes we had evidence that suggested the target area that would be the most likely source of such resistant material. We usually took advantage of having a collector in the field by having him collect everything on a "want" list for that area.

While many benefits have come from such explorations, they have contributed little to our knowledge of the total range of genetic diversity of a species and the distribution of that diversity ecogeographically. Neither did such collections permit the in-depth biosystematic/cytogenetic studies, in research centers far from the collection site, that could define gene flow (introgression) and gene frequencies on a population and areal basis. In short, they provided no reliable evidence on evolutionary aspects of the biotypes involved.

Now we are beginning to undertake ecogeographic studies of the target species in their areas of genetic diversity and to devise from these studies sampling strategies that will accommodate: 1) the objectives of germplasm conservation, and 2) other sampling strategies and site descriptions that will provide the basis for biosystematic studies and assessments of evolutionary trends (Qualset, 1975).

These ecogeographic studies involve multidisciplinary teams that can provide adequate characterization of soils, moisture regimens, biota, including beneficial and harmful microorganisms aboveground and in the rhizosphere.

With these rather intensive field studies, coupled with information derived from evaluation of collections already in gene banks, selective collection can be undertaken toward filling real gaps and toward reaching a level of knowledge that tells us when we have collected the genetic diversity of a species in a given area.

In cooperation with IPBGR, the Agricultural Research Service (ARS), USDA, has initiated an ecogeographic survey of genetic diversity of wheat and its wild relatives in eastern Turkey.

The technology of in vitro propagation and preservation of vegetative material is developing apace. We can expect that in the near future, we will be able to collect such material in the field, properly process it, and assure that it arrives at the laboratory of destination in good condition. This will permit selective collection of superior individual phenotypes of cross-pollinated, apomictic, or seed-sterile species.

MAINTENANCE

Maintenance or preservation of germplasm involves two principal considerations: (1) avoiding loss of genetic diversity and (2) avoiding costs.

We must maintain genetic diversity and do so at least cost. For whatever kind of germplasm being preserved, objective (1) is also priority 1. Long-term maintenance (base collections) provides the best set of circumstances for achieving these objectives. Regeneration, and hence, opportunity for genetic shift or loss, can be optimally minimized, while costly grow-outs can be avoided. Low temperature and low relative humidity (for all but a relatively few seeds) and good seed quality are prerequisites to good performance in storage.

Medium-term maintenance (active collections) is geared to meet the needs of the users of germplasm. The volume and frequency of use of these collections militate against the use of very low temperatures and very low relative humidities. Therefore, grow-outs for seed increase are relatively frequent and costly in terms of loss of diversity and of program resources. Here also the quality of the seed going into the gene bank has a lot to do with its performance in the maintenance environment.

It is obvious that we still have a great deal to learn about the interaction of seed genotypes and storage environments. Results contrary to expectations based on experience, keep cropping up; requiring us to continue monitoring viability on a too frequent schedule. This is very consumptive of seed, program resources, and probably of genetic resources and cries out for more research on the physiology of stored seeds. We are beginning to address these problems but we have a long way to go.

Maintenance of germplasm of clonally propagated crops demands a different set of requirements, for the most part. I say "for the most part" because genes of some clonally propagated crops can be maintained in backup seed and/or pollen collections. While these approaches make germplasm preservation more convenient and less costly, such gains are more than offset when germplasm preserved in these forms becomes the starting point for evaluation of parental stock, crossing, and selection in new variety development.

Tissue culture or in vitro storage followed by regeneration of plantlets or beds for scion stock may mitigate the inconvenience of not having gene banks like our present clonal repositories where mature plant specimens are maintained. These laboratory approaches to maintenance of germplasm of clonally propagated crops are being researched in numerous laboratories here and abroad (Withers, 1982).

In the last several years, there has been a considerable amount written about the need for "genetic reserves" (Mooney, 1977), "gene parks," "in situ" preservation, or "freezing our genes on the landscape." Since the tone of these articles has mostly been that in situ preservation should be in lieu of ex situ preservation, they have received generally negative responses from people who take germplasm preservation seriously. It is not difficult to list the drawbacks and hazards of relying on in situ gene banks for meeting preservation needs of germplasm of economic plants. Drawbacks such as locating the numerous sites that would be required for preserving the genetic diversity of only one broad-ranging and variable species let alone sites for some thousand species; accessibility of germplasm from such sites would not compare favorably with ex situ gene banks where controlled environments can permit location-for-convenience. Protection from such hazards as fire, storms, water, animals (including man and insects), other plants, and pathogens would have to be considered if we were to rely on in situ collections for meeting our germplasm needs. This could be expensive.

But the idea of in situ preservation should not be rejected without serious assessment. As a backup system to ex situ gene banks, it could offer benefits the latter cannot. One benefit may be products of continuing evolution—new genetic diversity. Another benefit, and probably of greater importance, is that they could be located and structurally designed (in terms of panmictic populations of modern varieties, landraces, and wild relatives) to provide field laboratories for the study of evolution of our crop plants.

EVALUATION

Evaluation of germplasm collections, it is generally agreed, holds highest priority among germplasm functions. It would be foolish to say that very little has been done in the way of germplasm evaluation. Tens and even hundreds of thousands of germplasm samples are sent out by the NPGS each year for some kind of evaluation by users. But where is the record, except in annual reports of curators where such numbers are tabulated? The record on reported results is embarrassingly small.

For the most part, we do not know what we are holding. So how can users or curators speak intelligently of "gaps" in collections? Or how can users do otherwise than ask for whole collections or major blocks of a collection? Without evaluation, our germplasm collections are of little use to plant breeders.

The Crop Advisory Committees have told us, crop-by-crop, what evaluations are of most use to the most users—the so-called minimum list of descriptors that they have developed. This is the evaluation work receiving the first organized attention through funding. But beyond that, we have to capture, through the Germplasm Resources Information Network (GRIN), organized data on all evaluation work carried out on NPGS material, at home and abroad. Also, we have to assist the communication and training that will help assure that meaningful data is taken and properly reported.

Agriculture Research Service has now entered into a cooperative program with Mexico to increase, evaluate, and maintain maize germplasm collections held in each country. Similar cooperative programs for maize are being implemented with Colombia and Peru.

ENHANCEMENT

Germplasm enhancement embraces those activities required to aggregate useful genes and gene combinations into usable phenotypes. These aggregates, or germplasm pools, could be considered as the feedstocks for varietal development programs. Eventually, the contributing sources of genes for such pools should be all germplasm within genetic reach.

Not all crops are at the same developmental level in terms of their needs for new sources of genetic diversity. Most breeders, I think it safe to say, agree that eventually more and more "exotic" germplasm will have to be mined for genetic diversity to meet the broadening diversity of user needs. We have started a limited program of germplasm enhancement, guided by recommendations of the Crop Advisory Committees, but much larger budgets are needed before we can expect progress that is at all proportional to the need.

VARIETAL DEVELOPMENT

The bottom line in justifying a germplasm program as described above is that the germplasm is used on farmers' fields to improve crop production efficiency and the quality of that product—be it food, feed, or fiber—in the marketplace. Plant breeders perform that all important job of putting genetic diversity into varietal packages that will take best advantage of given agricultural environments and market requirements.

This germplasm continuum—from collection in the wild to use on farmers' fields—has to be as effective as we can possibly make it if we are going to feed future world populations.

REFERENCES

1. Committee on Genetic Vulnerability of Major Crops. 1972. Genetic vulnerability of major crops. National Academy of Sciences, Washington, DC.

2. Hodge, W. H., and C. O. Erlanson. 1955. Plant introduction as a federal service to agriculture. Adv. Agron. 7:189–211.

3. Jones, Q., and S. Gillett. 1982. The NPGS (National Plant Germplasm System): An Overview. DIVERSITY, Spec. Rep. no. 1, Laboratory for Information Science in Agriculture, Fort Collins, CO.

4. Mooney, P. R. 1977. Seeds on the earth. Canadian Council for International Co-operation, Ottawa.

5. Qualset, C. O. 1975. Sampling germplasm in a center of diversity. p. 81–96. In O. H. Frankel and J. G. Hawkes (ed.) Crop genetic resources for today and tomorrow. Cambridge University Press, New York.

6. Ross, E. D. 1946. The United States Department of Agriculture during the Commissionership. Agric. History 20:132–133.

7. Smith, C. E., Jr. 1950. Prehistoric plant remains for bat cave. Bot. Mus. Leafl. Harvard Univ. 14:157–180.

8. Withers, L. 1982. Institutes Working on Tissue Culture for Genetic Conservation. A Consultant Report. International Board for Plant Genetic Resources. Rome, Italy.

Chapter 4

The Role and Experience of an International Crop-Specific Genetic Resources Center[1]

T. T. CHANG[2]

The crop improvement activities of the International Rice Research Institute (IRRI) encompass the complete range of genetic resources activities from acquisition to multidisciplinary evaluation, utilization, and long-term preservation. Thus, IRRI's role fulfills the Vavilovian concept of a plant genetic resources center (cf. Frankel, 1975), but its research programs are specific to rice (*Oryza sativa* L.) and rice-based farming systems. Orientation toward a single crop enables IRRI to focus on the basic needs of the crop, to effectively implement well-defined research objectives, and to perform a broad spectrum of services to rice researchers of the world (Chang et al., 1975a). On the other hand, the enormous genetic diversity existing in the genus *Oryza* (cf. Chang, 1976a, 1976b; Chang et al., 1982) has also presented unique challenges to both conservationists and the users.

In the face of continuous population increases in the major rice-consuming countries of Asia and Latin America, rice scientists will depend more and more on the available genetic resources to raise production levels and to stabilize crop yield. The demand for rice is continuously

[1] Contribution from the International Rice Germplasm Center (IRGC) at IRRI, P.O. Box 933, Manila, Philippines.

[2] Geneticist and head, the International Rice Germplasm Center, IRRI, P.O. Box 933, Manila, Philippines.

Copyright © 1984 Crop Science Society of America, 677 South Segoe Road, Madison, WI 53711. *Conservation of Crop Germplasm—An International Perspective.*

rising in many African countries where both the rice-growing environments and the indigenous cultigen (*O. glaberrima* Steud.) are distinct from those in Asia.

MISSION AND PRINCIPAL ACTIVITIES OF THE IRGC

To concretize the vision of the founders of IRRI (Chandler, 1963) and to meet the demand of rice breeders (IRRI, 1972), the International Rice Germplasm Center (IRGC) at IRRI has been given the mandate of conserving the world's rice genetic resources for unrestricted use by rice researchers and growers. The primary functions of the Center are:

— to acquire a full spectrum of rice germplasm in the genus *Oryza* (cf. Chang et al., 1979) by coordinated field collection and systematic exchange,

— to systematically characterize conserved accessions of cultivated and wild species,

— to preserve the seed stocks of the base collection under ideal storage conditions at IRRI and at duplicate sites, and

— to supply seed and related information to rice workers for further improvement of the crop.

The staff of the Center trains rice conservationists, develops manuals for field collection (Chang et al., 1972) and management of the conserved resources (Chang, 1976c), implements seed storage studies, and advises national centers on seed storage facilities and procedure (Rockefeller Foundation, 1980).

The IRRI's collaboration with the International Board for Plant Genetic Resources (IBPGR) resulted in a Rice Advisory Committee which prepares plans and advises the international centers and national centers on broad subjects of common concern (cf. Chang, 1980). A set of uniform descriptors was developed by the Committee (IBPGR-IRRI Rice Advisory Committee, 1980). Guidelines for conserving the Asian wild species also stemmed from field studies of the group (IBPGR-IRRI Rice Advisory Committee, 1982).

Since acquisition and seed multiplication activities began on a modest scale in late 1961, the IRGC staff has carried out continually expanding activities in the following areas:

1. Seed Collection. Existing collections in national and state centers have been systematically acquired. Other international and regional agricultural research centers in Africa and Latin America have provided IRRI with duplicate sets of their recent collections. The IRGC coordinates worldwide collection activities and participates in assembling uncollected germplasm from remote corners of the world. Botanists, anthropologists, missionaries, and service volunteers have helped in collection activities in nearly inaccessible areas (Chang, 1980; Chang et al., 1982b). The IRRI and IBPGR jointly sponsored workshops in 1977 and 1983 to develop 5-year plans for major ecogeographic rice regions (IRRI-IBPGR, 1978, 1983).

During 1971 to 1982, IRRI staff joined national workers in canvassing germplasm-rich areas in seven Asian countries and collected 10 472 seed samples. Workers of national and other agencies in another seven countries of tropical Asia assembled 25 528 additional samples with some technical or financial assistance provided by IRRI. Since 1979, the IBPGR has provided financial assistance to field collectors in national programs through a network coordinated by IRRI.

The role of IRGC in field conservation is both catalytic and synergistic. By stimulating local interest and pooling resources from many agencies and donors (Chang and Perez, 1975; IRRI-IBPGR, 1978, 1983), the collection campaign gained great momentum and attained unprecedented dimensions. The overall deposits have increased IRRI's holding from 14 712 accessions of *O. sativa* in 1971 (Chang, 1972) to 67 000 accessions in mid-1983. The IRGC also maintains 2600 African cultivars (*O. glaberrima*), 1100 populations of wild species, and 690 genetic testers and mutants. The total holding makes IRRI's viable seedstocks the world's largest collection for a single crop. About 9000 of these accessions reputedly have tolerance or resistance to environmental or biotic stresses in specific ecological niches (Chang, 1980). Collection efforts have not only saved numerous traditional varieties from genetic wipe-out, but also greatly enriched the germplasm available for research purposes.

2. Seed Preservation. A well-constructed, medium-term seed storage room (2 to 3°C) has been available for seed storage since 1961. The cold storage facility freed the IRGC staff from the task of growing the entire collection every year—a crushing load on the staff of many centers in the humid tropics not having adequate cold storage facilities. Since 1980, the seed stocks are stored in short-term (19 to 20°C, 50% relative humidity, RH), medium-term (2 to 3°C, 40% RH), long-term (−10°C, 35% RH) rooms, with projected seed longevity of 3 to 5, 30 to 40 and more than 70 years, respectively. For medium- and long-term storages, the seeds are dried to 6% moisture content by a special drying process and hermetically sealed under partial vacuum in aluminum cans (IRRI, 1980). A duplicate set of freshly harvested seed samples is deposited at the U.S. National Seed Storage Laboratory (NSSL) at Fort Collins, CO for added security.

The IRRI also cooperates with the National Institute of Agricultural Sciences (NIAS) of Japan, the U.S. Department of Agriculture (USDA), the International Institute of Tropical Agriculture (IITA), and the West Africa Rice Development Association (WARDA) in consolidating and exchanging collections for storage at duplicate sites. The overall aim is to provide additional security for irreplaceable germplasm.

3. Characterization. A set of 45 morpho-agronomic traits is systematically recorded for each accession (IRRI-IBPGR Rice Advisory Committee, 1980). The data are entered in computerized files and are readily available for retrieval (IRRI, 1970; Gomez et al., 1979). When an accession is being rejuvenated for seed renewal, the data are used to verify the identity of the stock.

The morpho-agronomic data, together with the 39-item data files on such economic (Genetic Evaluation and Utilization, GEU) traits as disease and insect reactions, are frequently retrieved to help rice researchers in obtaining appropriate test materials.

4. Seed Increase. The IRGC personnel plant, record, and harvest 12 ha of plantings each crop season for seed multiplication, systematic characterization, and seed rejuvenation. The massive operations are carried out on staggered dates by seasonally oriented schedules, amounting to 25 ha/year.

5. Seed Distribution. The provision of seed and related agronomic data is a major service function of the Center. The IRGC serves as an exchange center for rice germplasm, not only among nations, but among different disciplines of rice research. Assistance to workers in marginal production areas where ecologic constraints exist frequently requires both computer and library searches. During the last 10 years about 5500 seed samples were annually sent abroad gratis in response to an average of about 150 requests a year. The IRRI itself uses between 20 500 and 50 400 samples from the bank each year (IRRI, 1983). Since its inception the IRGC has provided more than 500 000 seed packets to rice researchers.

6. Seed Restoration to Donors. Thousands of accessions have been returned to national and state centers when the varieties were no longer grown in the donor country or were unavailable in viable form from local depositories. A unique example of this service is the recent return of major commercial varieties to strife-torn Kampuchea (IRRI, 1982a).

Timeliness in expanding and improving IRRI's germplasm activities and facilities has been a key factor in enabling IRRI to cope with the rapid change in germplasm replacement or disappearance (Chang, 1980).

LINKAGE BETWEEN GERMPLASM EVALUATION AND USE

Investments in genetic conservation may not be justified unless the conserved materials are fully evaluated and used. It was a fortunate development that IRRI scientists began screening accessions in the germplasm bank for agronomic promise and tolerance for various biotic stresses soon after IRRI was established. The first breakthrough was the development of IR8 with the incorporation of the semidwarf gene (sd_1) into the background of tropical varieties (cf. Chandler, 1968).

The IRRI plant pathologists tested thousands of accessions for resistance to the blast fungus (*Pyricularia oryzae* Cavara), the bacterial blight pathogen (*Xanthomonas oryzae* Uyeda and Ishiyama), and, later insect-transmitted viruses. Entomologists evaluated equally large collections for reactions to stem borers (*Chilo* spp. and *Sesamia* spp.), the green leafhopper (*Nephotettix* spp.), and the brown planthopper (*Nilaparvata* spp.). Plant physiologists tested many early maturing varieties for tolerance to cool temperatures. Cereal chemists compared the protein and lysine contents of tropical varieties. Soil chemists compared varietal reactions when one or more adverse soil factors (salinity, alkalinity, Zn deficiency, Fe deficiency, and Fe toxicity) were present. Geneticists and agronomists screened different segments of the germplasm collection for drought resistance. Results of the massive evaluation activities between 1962 and 1974 have been summarized by IRRI staff (Ou, 1972; Pathak, 1972; Juliano, 1972; Chang et al., 1974, 1975b; Ponnamperuma, 1977).

The multidisciplinary evaluation efforts were expanded and systematized during 1974 as the GEU program of IRRI (Brady, 1975). The interdisciplinary and problem-oriented coordination between plant breeders and "problem-area" scientists in allied disciplines received sharper focus and direction under the GEU program. The operational aspects of the program have been described elsewhere (IRRI, 1974; Chang et al., 1982a). The team approach has resulted in greater research inputs from all individual members and fuller use of improved germplasm.

One of the major focuses under the GEU program is to develop rices that can cope with biological and physiological constraints in unfavored rice production areas. Farmers in such areas were bypassed by modern technology associated with semidwarf rices and access to irrigation water. The unfavored production areas embrace the following non-irrigated culture types: shallow rainfed-lowland, rainfed-upland, medium-deepwater, deepwater, and tidal swamp rices. Rice growers in such areas represent nearly three-fourths of these of tropical Asia (IRRI, 1976a). An example of such efforts to cope with rice production in drought-prone areas was recently discussed by Chang et al. (1982a).

The IRGC has provided the bulk of the genetic materials for the massive testing phase of the GEU program. Certain GEU tests are accelerated when the germplasm staff supplies newly acquired seeds of accessions reputed to have special characteristics to the GEU scientists concerned, so as to speed up the evaluation process. Special characteristics include floating ability, tolerance for cool temperatures, and adverse soil factors. Japanese breeders on Hokkaido Island have identified the cv. Silewah (Acc. 25718) of north Sumatra (Indonesia) as the most cold tolerant entry among cultivars collected from high elevations (Satake and Toriyama, 1979). Several saline-resistant accessions were collected from salty areas in India and Sri Lanka. Rodent's avoidance of "bitter stalk" varieties of Indonesia was confirmed.

The increase in the magnitude of the GEU program is indicated by the increasing numbers of seed requests submitted by IRRI scientists and supplied by the IRGC: from 66 seed requests in 1973 and 319 requests in 1981 (IRRI, 1983). The number of seed requests is roughly equivalent to the number of evaluation experiments.

The IRRI's success in evaluating and using rice germplasm has encouraged several major national rice research centers in Asia to set up national GEU programs. The forerunner of such national programs is the All-India Coordinated Rice Improvement Project.

During 1975 to 1977, resistant or tolerant accessions from the IRGC also furnished a substantial portion of the test materials in the nurseries of the International Rice Testing Program (IRTP) coordinated by IRRI.

IMPACT ON RICE IMPROVEMENT

Nearly all of the national and state centers besides China have made profitable use of the sd_1 gene contributed by Dee-geo-woo-gen (Hargrove, 1978). Chinese rice breeders have used two semidwarf sources which shared the same locus as sd_1 (Chang and Li, 1980; Shen, 1980).

A large number of outstanding sources of other desirable traits have been identified among the IRRI accessions and have subsequently been used through the multidisciplinary efforts of IRRI's GEU teams and rice researchers of different rice-growing countries (cf. Chang et al., 1982b). Some desirable traits and their outstanding sources are cited below to show the dividends from a large germplasm bank when the conserved stocks are effectively evaluated and used.

1. Resistance to tungro virus: Pankhari 203, Gampai 15, PTB10, PTB18, and other varieties.

2. Resistance to grassy stunt virus: one strain of *O. nivara* (IRRI Acc. 101508) from Uttar Pradesh/State, India.

3. Resistance to ragged stunt virus: wild relatives of *O. sativa*, one of which came from Taiwan and is now extinct there.

4. Resistance to the brown planthopper (*N. lugens* Stl.): Mudgo, ASD7, Triveni, Utri Rajapan, TKM6, and other varieties.

5. Resistance to the whitebacked planthopper (*Sogatella furcifera* Horvath): N22, PTB19, Podiwi-A8, and others.

6. Tolerance for salinity: Pokkali, Getu, Dasal, Nona Bokra, and others.

7. Tolerance for submergence: FR13A, FR43A, Goda Heenati, Kurkaruppan, and others.

8. Drought resistance: Moroberekan, OS4, 63-83, Black Gora, Dular, IAC47, and others.

9. Tolerance for cool temperatures: Leng Kwang and Silewah.

10. Heavy grain weight: upland varieties of Laos and Thailand.

11. Cytoplasmic male-sterility (CMS): Taichung Native 1. Another useful source is *O. ativa* f. *spontanea* (Wild Aborted) of China. The IRRI assisted many rice breeders in gaining access to the Chinese CMS lines.

The increase in rice production between 1965 and 1980 amounted to 120 million tons, to which the improved varieties have contributed about 27.37 million tons. The varietal component is valued at about 4.5 billion dollars (Herdt and Capule, 1983). The contribution of the new varieties has already paid many times over the costs of assembling and maintaining the rice collection at IRRI—(about $500 000 in 1983).

The IRRI has been uniquely successful in using rice germplasm mainly because the rice genetic resources program is an integral component of its multidisciplinary rice improvement (GEU) program. Moreover, this author also uses genetic resources for both genetic studies and breeding purposes and is thus keenly aware of the research needs of rice breeders and problem area scientists. Effective communication between the germplasm curator and the users is essential for efficient use of the germplasm resources.

Seeds drawn from the IRGC have enabled IRRI scientists and many researchers elsewhere to conduct in-depth investigations on the rice plant and on varietal differences, which in the long run have contributed significantly to rice research and yield improvement. A wealth of information has been obtained on the ecological aspects of rice production, physico-chemical aspects of the grain and its development, photoperiod response, temperature stresses, water deficit, submergence response, resistance to insects and viruses, and tolerance for adverse soil factors.

Genetic and cytogenetic studies have clarified allelic relationships among genes for semidwarfism, biotic tolerances, and affinity among varietal groups. The publications are too numerous to be enumerated here, but IRRI has published a series of monographs on different subjects (IRRI, 1965, 1969, 1972, 1975, 1976b, 1978, 1979a, 1979b, 1979c, 1979d, 1979e, 1982b, 1982c). Reviews on genetical studies and progress in breeding are also available (Chang and Vergara, 1972; Vergara and Chang, 1976; Chang and Oka, 1976; Khush, 1977; Chang and Li, 1980).

CONSTRAINTS ON CONSERVATION AND RESOURCES MANAGEMENT

Although the IRGC has been endowed with adequate support, fine facilities, use-oriented services, a dedicated staff, continuity in management, and excellent working relationship with colleagues in national rice research programs and other international centers, we have encountered increasing constraints, especially because the collection continues to grow and, at the same time, the bulk of the older seed stocks (about 44 500 accessions) needs to be rejuvenated and processed for medium- and long-term storage by the vacuum canning procedure. The major constraints on field collection, seed preservation, plant health monitoring, and seed distribution are enumerated below:

1. Field exploration and assemblage of cultivars. Field collection is a time-consuming and arduous task. Canvassing and sampling during the monsoon season by a small team can cover only a limited area. Because of politico-military strifes, many areas in tropical Asia are not accessible to field collectors.

2. Wild species. Only small segments of the wild taxa have been conserved. The collection of wild species requires trained workers, and the maintenance phase is very demanding. Conserving the wild taxa in natural reserves is impractical.

3. Genetic identity of cultivars. Many accessions represent mixtures of cultivars. Others represent single cultivars having several different names and some accessions have lost their characteristic features. It is difficult to differentiate among: probable duplicates, eco-strains and morphologic variants having the same or similar names. Both biochemical and biometrical techniques are needed to sort out duplicates.

4. Seed production. All land races and old varieties are low yielding. Poor adaptation to the IRRI environment or susceptibility to locally prevalent pests further reduces seed yield or even endangers the perpetuation of the seed stocks. We are also conscious of the pitfalls of frequent rejuvenation in small plots (Chang et al., 1979).

5. Plant quarantine problems. The IRRI enjoys great freedom in introducing and exporting rice seeds, but grave responsibilities with respect to plant quarantine also rest with IRRI staff. The IRRI needs to strengthen its plant health monitoring measures. International seed exchanges are sometimes handicapped by uncooperative plant quarantine officers or lack of facilities for handling the introductions.

6. Seed preservation. We have established that there is differential seed longevity among varieties of diverse origin. It is difficult to monitor

the viability of every accession in our center. Moreover, every germination test means the loss of a certain number of seeds from the small seed stocks. The long-term effects of disease infection and fumigation on seed longevity need to be determined.

7. Seed distribution. We cannot predict the demand for seeds. An accession becomes very much in demand when it shows certain desirable features after evaluation. Then the existing seed stock becomes insufficient to meet all requests. We are obliged to supply 20 g seed of each cultivar and 10 to 20 seeds per wild taxon. Sometimes, we do a special seed increase for a researcher if time and field space allow.

8. Duplicate sites of preservation. We have been striving for duplicate sites of preservation. Our collaborative efforts with the NIAS and USDA have been mentioned. Other centers also have constraints of space, personnel, and related support.

DIRECTIONS FOR FUTURE ENDEAVOR

As an international crop genetic resources center, the IRGC will continually expand and improve its efforts in the following areas:

1. Field collection. A workshop to develop a second 5-year plan was recently held at IRRI (IRRI-IBPGR, 1983). With joint inputs from national programs, other international or regional centers, IBPGR, and IRRI, field activities will be accelerated towards completion of the assembling of local germplasm from accessible areas. The IBPGR has recently posted an advisor at IRRI to assist in field collection. Acquisition of recent collections made elsewhere will be sought.

2. Characterization and identification. Biochemical and biometrical techniques are being studied to develop additional criteria for differentiating duplicate samples and for identifying questionable accessions.

3. Seed production. A seed increase site away from IRRI and relatively free from epidemics is being used for seed rejuvenation. The proportion of healthy seeds that could be produced is higher than on the IRRI farm.

4. Seed preservation. Additional experiments on seed treatments, containers, and storage conditions will be initiated toward the improvement of storage methods, especially for national centers. Technical assistance to allow national centers to improve their seed storage facilities will be continued or expanded.

5. Training program. In addition to short-term training to accommodate different needs, a formalized training course and degree programs will be added.

6. Interinstitutional cooperation. The IRRI will continue to negotiate measures which will facilitate an expanded and systematic collaboration with other centers such as the USDA and NIAS so that duplicate samples can be stored at more than one location and so that rejuvenation of seeds of unadapted accessions can be carried out at other locations. The IRRI can reciprocate by providing similar assistance to NIAS and other centers.

The above measures are designed to continuously provide gene resources for further improvement of the crop, to reinstate its genetic diversity, and to stabilize yield under various stresses. New sources of desirable traits are needed to cope with the ever-rising number of insect pests and diseases (Chang, 1984) and to expand rice production into new areas where exotic fauna and flora and soil and water conditions may act as constraints to profitable production. The need to effectively use the remarkably diverse rice germplasm becomes more urgent as human population increases in developing countries continue to outstrip per capita food production gains despite the advances of rice production made during the last 20 years (IFPRI, 1977; Hsieh et al., 1982; IRRI, 1982d).

REFERENCES

1. Brady, N. C. 1975. Rice responds to science. p. 62–96. In A. W. A. Brown et al. (ed.) Crop productivity—Research imperatives. Kettering Foundation, Cleveland, OH.

2. Chandler, R. F., Jr. 1963. The International Rice Research Institute. p. 67–70. In Symposium on rice problems (Proc. 10th Pacific Sci. Congr., University of Hawaii, 21 Aug.–6 Sept. 1961), Int. Rice Comm. Newsl. Spec. Issue.

3. ————. 1968. Dwarf rice—a giant in tropical Asia. p. 252–255. In Science for better living (The Yearbook of Agriculture, 1968). U.S. Department of Agriculture, Washington, DC.

4. Chang, T. T. 1972. International cooperation in conserving and evaluating rice germplasm resources. p. 177–185. In Rice breeding. IRRI, Los Baños, Philippines.

5. ————. 1976a. The rice cultures. In The early history of agriculture. Philos. Trans. R. Soc. London B275:421–441.

6. ————. 1976b. The origin, evolution, cultivation, dissemination, and diversification of Asian and African rices. Euphytica 25:425–441.

7. ————. 1976c. Manual on genetic conservation of rice germplasm for evaluation and utilization. IRRI, Los Baños, Philippines.

8. ————. 1980. The rice genetic resources program of IRRI and its impact on rice improvement. p. 85–105. In Rice improvement in China and other Asian countries. IRRI, Los Baños, Philippines.

9. ————. 1984. Conservation of rice genetic resources: Luxury or necessity? Science 224: 251–256.

10. ————, C. R. Adair, and T. H. Johnston. 1982b. The conservation and use of rice genetic resources. Adv. Agron. 35:37–91.

11. ————, W. L. Brown, J. Sneep, J. G. Boonman, and H. Lamberts. 1979. Crop genetic resources. p. 83–103. In J. Sneep and A. J. T. Hendriksen (ed.) Plant breeding perspectives, PUDOC, Wageningen.

12. ————, and C. C. Li. 1980. Genetics and breeding. p. 87–146. In B. S. Luh (ed.) Rice: Production and utilization. AVI, Westport, Conn.

13. ————, G. C. Loresto, J. C. O'Toole, and J. L. Armenta-Soto. 1982a. Strategy and methodology of breeding rice for drought-prone areas. p. 217–244. In Drought resistance in crops with emphasis on rice. IRRI, Los Baños, Philippines.

14. ————, ————, and O. Tagumpay. 1974. Screening rice germplasm for drought resistance. SABRAO J. 6(1):9–16.

15. ————, and H. I. Oka. 1976. Genetic variousness in the climatic adaptation of rice cultivars. p. 87–111. In Climate and rice. IRRI, Los Baños, Philippines.

16. ————, S.H. Ou, M. D. Pathak, K. C. Ling, and H. E. Kauffman. 1975b. The search for disease and insect resistance in rice germplasm. p. 183–200. In O. H. Frankel and J. G. Hawkes (ed.) Crop genetic resources for today and tomorrow. Cambridge University Press, New York.

17. ———, and A. T. Perez. 1975. Genetic conservation of rice germplasm in South East and South Asia, 1971–74. p. 120–128. *In* J. T. Williams et al. (ed.) South East Asian plant genetic resources. IBPGR-BIOTROP-LBN, Bogor, Indonesia.

18. ———, S. D. Sharma, C. R. Adair, and A. T. Perez. 1972. Manual for field collectors of rice. IRRI, Los Baños, Philippines.

19. ———, and B. S. Vergara. 1972. Ecological and genetic information on adaptability and yielding ability in tropical rice varieties. p. 431–452. *In* Rice breeding. IRRI, Los Baños, Philippines.

20. ———, R. L. Villareal, G. C. Loresto, and A. T. Perez. 1975a. IRRI's role as a genetic resources centre. p. 457–466. *In* O. H. Frankel and J. G. Hawkes (ed.) Crop genetic resources for today and tomorrow. Cambridge University Press, New York.

21. Frankel, O. H. 1975. Genetic resources centres—A cooperative global network. p. 473–481. *In* O. H. Frankel and J. G. Hawkes (ed.) Crop genetic resources for today and tomorrow. Cambridge University Press, New York.

22. Gomez, K. A., D. Tuazon, and N. E. Nano. 1979. Germplasm bank information retrieval system. IRRI Res. Paper Ser. 45.

23. Hargrove, T. R. 1978. Diffusion and adoption of gene materials among rice breeding programs in Asia. IRRI Res. Paper Ser. 18.

24. Herdt, R. W., and C. Capule. 1983. Adoption, spread and production impact of modern rice varieties in Asia. IRRI, Los Baños, Philippines.

25. Hsieh, S. C., J. C. Flinn, and N. Amerasinghe. 1982. The role of rice in meeting future needs. p. 27–49. *In* Rice research strategies for the future. IRRI, Los Baños, Philippines.

26. IBPGR-IRRI Rice Advisory Committee. 1980. Descriptors for rice (*Oryza sativa* L.). IRRI, Los Baños, Philippines.

27. ———. 1982. Conservation of the wild rices of tropical Asia. Plant Genetic Resour. Newsl. 49:13–18.

28. IFPRI. 1977. Food needs of developing countries: projections of production and consumption to 1990. IFPRI Res. Rep. no. 3. Washington, DC.

29. IRRI. 1965. Mineral nutrition of the rice plant. Johns Hopkins Press, Baltimore, MD.

30. ———. 1969. Virus diseases of the rice plant. Johns Hopkins Press, Baltimore, MD.

31. ———. 1970. Catalog of rice cultivars and breeding lines (*Oryza sativa* L.) in the world collection of the International Rice Research Institute. IRRI, Los Baños, Philippines.

32. ———. 1972. Rice breeding. IRRI, Los Baños, Philippines.

33. ———. 1974. IRRI's GEU program: Tapping the genetic reservoir of rice. IRRI Reporter 2/74.

34. ———. 1975. Major research in upland rice. IRRI, Los Baños, Philippines.

35. ———. 1976a. Annual report for 1975. IRRI, Los Baños, Philippines.

36. ———. 1976b. Climate and rice. IRRI, Los Baños, Philippines.

37. ———. 1978. Soils and rice. IRRI, Los Baños, Philippines.

38. ———. 1979a. Proceedings of the rice blast workshop. IRRI, Los Baños, Philippines.

39. ———. 1979b. Chemical aspects of rice grain quality. IRRI, Los Baños, Philippines.

40. ———. 1979c. Report of a rice cold tolerance workshop. IRRI, Los Baños, Philippines.

41. ———. 1979d. Brown planthopper: Threat to rice production in Asia. IRRI, Los Baños, Philippines.

42. ———. 1979e. Rainfed lowland rice: Selected papers from the 1978 International Rice Research Conference. IRRI, Los Baños, Philippines.

43. ———. 1980. IRRI Germplasm Bank—A treasure of mankind. IRRI Reporter 3/80.

44. ———. 1982a. IRRI germplasm bank returns traditional rice seeds to Kampuchea. IRRI Reporter 3/82.

45. ———. 1982b. Drought resistance in crops with emphasis on rice. IRRI, Los Baños, Philippines.

46. ———. 1982c. Proceedings of the 1981 International Deepwater Rice Workshop. IRRI, Los Baños, Philippines.

47. ----. 1982d. Annual report for 1981. IRRI, Los Baños, Philippines.

48. ----. 1983. Annual report for 1982. IRRI, Los Baños, Philippines.

49. IRRI-IBPGR. 1978. Proceedings of the Workshop on the Genetic Conservation of Rice. IRRI, Los Baños, Philippines.

50. ----. 1983. Proceedings of the Second Workshop on Rice Germplasm Conservation. IRRI, Los Baños, Philippines.

51. Juliano, B. O. 1972. Physicochemical properties of starch and protein in relation to grain quality and nutritional value of rice. p. 389–404. *In* Rice breeding. IRRI, Los Baños, Philippines.

52. Khush, G. S. 1977. Disease and insect resistance in rice. Adv. Agron. 29:265–341.

53. Ou, S. H. 1972. Rice diseases. Commonwealth Mycological Institute, Kew, Surrey, England.

54. Pathak, M. D. 1972. Varietal resistance to rice stemborers at IRRI. p. 405–418. *In* The major insect pests of the rice plant. Johns Hopkins Press, Baltimore, MD.

55. Ponnamperuma, F. N. 1977. Screening rice for tolerance to mineral stresses. IRRI Res. Paper Series 6.

56. Rockefeller Foundation. 1980. Crop germplasm conservation and use in China. Rockefeller Foundation, New York.

57. Satake, T., and K. Toriyama. 1979. Two extremely cool-tolerant varieties. Int. Rice Res. Newsl. 4(2):9–10.

58. Shen, J. H. 1980. Rice breeding in China. p. 9–30. *In* Rice improvement in China and other Asian countries. IRRI, Los Baños, Philippines.

59. Vergara, B. S., and T. T. Chang. 1976. The flowering response of the rice plant to photoperiod. IRRI, Los Baños, Philippines.

Chapter 5

International Germplasm Collection, Conservation, and Exchange at ICRISAT[1]

MELAK H. MENGESHA[2]

Germplasm is the most important raw material for any crop improvement program, and yet humankind continues to be faced with the extinction of this invaluable and irreplaceable resource. One of the best descriptions of genetic resources is given by Mehra and Arora (16) who stated, "Plant genetic resources represent the sum total of diversity accumulated through years of evolution under domestication and natural selection". Genetic manipulation (3) is advancing at a fast pace and the process may be even more accelerated by the application of genetic engineering techniques. But nothing can be achieved, even by genetic engineering, unless those desirable genes are at our disposal. Jain (11) considered germplasm as part of human biological heritage without whose free exchange present-day farm productivity would not have been possible. In this regard, the International Agricultural Research Centers strategically located at regions of rich crop diversity are in a unique position to collect and conserve germplasm and make it readily available to all scientists throughout the world.

[1] Contribution from the International Crops Research Institute for the Semi-Arid Tropics, Andhra Pradesh, India.

[2] Principal germplasm botanist and leader, Genetic Resources Unit, International Crops Research Institute for the Semi-Arid Tropics (ICRISAT), Patancheru P.O. 502 324, Andhra Pradesh, India.

Copyright © 1984 Crop Science Society of America, 677 South Segoe Road, Madison, WI 53711. *Conservation of Crop Germplasm—An International Perspective.*

In the area of genetic resources, International Crops Research Institute for the Semi-Arid Tropics' (ICRISAT) major objectives are to:

1. Collect and assemble the germplasm of the cultivated and wild relatives of its mandated crops, namely:

Sorghum	— *Sorghum bicolor* (Linn.) Moench
Pearl millet	— *Pennisetum americanum* (L.) Leeke
Pigeon pea	— *Cajanus cajan* (L.) Huth
Chickpea	— *Cicer arietinum* (L.)
Groundnut	— *Arachis hypogaea* (L.)

The institute also collects and conserves the germplasm of the following six minor millets:

Finger millet	— *Eleusine coracana* (L.) Gaertn.
Foxtail millet	— *Setaria italica* (L.) P. Beauv.
Proso millet	— *Panicum miliaceum* L.
Little millet	— *P. sumatrense* Roth
Barnyard millet	— *Echinochloa crusgalli* (L.) P. Beauv.
Kodo millet	— *Paspalum scrobiculatum* L.

2. Characterize, evaluate, and document the germplasm.
3. Maintain and rejuvenate the germplasm without marked alteration of the original genotype or mixture of genotypes.
4. Serve as a world repository of the germplasm of ICRISAT mandated crops and the six minor millets by conserving the germplasm in medium and long-term cold storage.
5. Distribute and exchange germplasm for present and future utilization.

GERMPLASM COLLECTION

Germplasm collection has lately gained due recognition. However, actual collection work is still lagging behind. If we are to avert food shortages and subsequent famines, we have to accelerate crop improvement programs, starting with collection and conservation of vanishing germplasm. The problem of food shortage and the need for urgent crop improvement programs is most alarming in the developing world. However, it is in the developing countries where the greatest diversity of our germplasm still exists, although it is gradually dwindling. Furthermore, germplasm in itself does not provide higher productivity. It needs to be explored and utilized more effectively in crop improvement programs under different environmental conditions. The time to collect the traditional landraces is now, before they are replaced by newly bred, high-yielding cultivars (5). In some cases it is already too late (17).

One source of concern is that many germplasm collection missions have been launched at about the prime maturity time of the crops to be collected. As a result, the farmers have often already harvested and consumed most of the early maturing types. We have to change our collection strategies so that we will be able to collect sufficient samples of early maturing types that may prove vital in averting future famines. The success of any germplasm collection mission largely depends on the collector's

Table 1. Germplasm collection, conservation, and distribution at ICRISAT
(as of 1 May 1983).

Crop	No. of accessions con- served	No. of samples in transit	No. of accessions evaluated	No. of com- puterized accessions	No. of samples dis- tributed	No. of wild relatives main- tained	No. of countries repre- sented
Sorghum	22 898	2 175	19 363	7 114	184 025	278	79
Pearl millet	16 002	--	15 388	924	37 944	20	30
Pigeon pea	9 936	345	9 930	9 697	54 836	38	33
Chickpea	12 950	--	12 200	11 000	103 899	14	40
Groundnut	10 248	2 017	9 190	174	33 859	21	80
Six minor millets	4 512	451	4 295	--	19 493	6	31
Total:	76 546	4 988	70 366	28 909	434 056	377	--

Table 2. Range of variation in 12 selected characters of sorghum and pearl millet
germplasm evaluated at ICRISAT Center, Patancheru.

Character	Range of variation	
	Sorghum	Pearl millet
Days to 50% flowering	36–199	33–140
Plant height (cm)	55–655	35–475
Peduncle exertion (cm)	0–55	$-21-+30$
Midrib color	White-brown	White-purple
Head length (cm)	2.5–71	6–165
Head width (cm)	1–29	1–6.4
Glume color	Straw-black	Straw-purple
Glume covering	Exposed-covered	Exposed-covered
Grain color	White-dark brown	White-dark brown
100 grain weight (g)	0.58–8.5	0.3–1.4
Tillering (no.)	1–15	1–210
Sugar content %	12–38	4.9–19.7

knowledge of the crops, their wild relatives, geographical and political accessibility, proper collection strategies, correct sampling procedures, safe and rapid transfer of the collected material, and timely evaluation and utilization.

The numbers of germplasm accessions assembled by ICRISAT from various countries and samples distributed to several countries are summarized in Table 1. Detailed information is given in the 1980 and 1981 Annual Reports of ICRISAT (8, 9). For each of the ICRISAT crops, these accessions represent the largest collection of germplasm assembled at any one place. However, considering the extent of the area devoted to these crops, the present collection is still too small.

The importance of the collected and conserved germplasm depends in part on its genetic diversity. The range of variation in some selected characters of sorghum and pearl millet is given in Table 2. A wide range of variation is also available for pigeon pea, chickpea (Table 3), and groundnut (Table 4). The range of variation was even higher for chickpea evaluated at Hissar, Hayana, India (21). Likewise, a wider range of variation was recorded when 343 pearl millet collections were evaluated

Table 3. Range of variation in 15 selected characters of pigeon pea and chickpea
germplasm evaluated at ICRISAT Center, Patancheru.

Character	Range of variation	
	Chickpea	Pigeon pea
Growth habit	erect-semi-spreading	compact-spreading
Stem color	green-purple	green-purple
Flower color	white-blue	ivory-purple
Seed color	cream-black	white-black
Seed shape	angular-globular	oval-square
Days to 50% flowering	28–96	55–228
Days to maturity	90–137	105–260
Primary branch per plant (no.)	--	2–66
Secondary branch per plant (no.)	--	0.3–145
Raceme per plant (no.)	--	10–788
Plant height (cm)	16–93	39–400
Plant width (cm)	18–70	--
No. of pods per plant	few–168	--
Seed per pod	1–2.8	2–8.5
100 seed weight (g)	4.9–59.4	2.8–26.5

Table 4. Range of variation in 13 selected characters of groundnut germplasm
evaluated at ICRISAT Center, Patancheru.

Character	Range of variation
Days to 50% flowering	16–58
Days to maturity	75–155
Length of reproductive branch (mm)	8–122
Leaflet length (mm)	24–86
Leaflet width (mm)	8–41
Pod length (mm)	11–60
Pod diameter (mm)	9–27
No. of seeds per pod	1–5
Seed color	Off-white–Dark purple
Seed length (mm)	7–21
Seed width (mm)	5–13
100 seed weight (g)	19.8–121.5
Oil content (%)	31.8–53.1

in a multi-locational evaluation program conducted in India and West
Africa.

The main purpose of pointing out the range of variation is to under-
line the importance of collection and exchange of the diverse germplasm
that may otherwise be lost. Although, the conserved variation is very
useful, it is yet considered small compared to what is available in nature.
Unfortunately, its availability in nature cannot be guaranteed in view of
the alarming genetic erosion that is taking place around the world. A
good example of such genetic erosion is the complete absence of "zera
zera" and "Hegari" sorghum landraces in the Geziera Province of Sudan,
and their replacement by the newly bred cultivars (17).

CONSERVATION

The problem of seed conservation probably started soon after we
domesticated crops about 10 000 to 12 000 years ago (5). Until recent
years, crop improvement scientists did not much care if their collected

germplasm were lost, because they could find and recollect such seeds easily (6). Now, there is strong evidence that it is not always easy to find the landraces where they were seen last. If plant breeders want to have a ready supply of germplasm, the time has come for them to rely on man made gene banks. Maintenance and preservation of landraces in protected gene reserves, though desirable in some specific cases, may not be practical or economical. Moreover, safety and continuity cannot be always assured. Therefore, we do not seem to have any other alternative but to collect urgently and conserve our invaluable germplasm in genebanks.

At ICRISAT, over 74 000 germplasm accessions of the institute's mandated crops are now conserved in medium-term (+ 4°C and about 30% relative humidity) cold storage facilities. About 500 g·seed of each accession is dried to about 5 to 7% moisture before it is stored. The type of storage chambers used at ICRISAT and the general standards and systems of germplasm technology and conservation have been described by Mengesha and Rao (17) and the IBPGR (10), respectively. More comprehensive reports on viability of seeds and principles and practices of seed storage are given by Roberts (20) and Justice and Bass (12). Long-term cold storage (− 20°C) chambers have been ordered and will soon be installed as part of the ICRISAT gene bank. The latest germination test on conserved seeds showed over 92% viability after years of storage. All the stored seeds are rejuvenated before their germination drops below 85% or before the seed quantity reaches a critical level.

It must be stressed here that only those seeds that are harvested from disease-free plants are conserved in the gene bank. Stringent field inspections and laboratory tests are made to ensure storage and distribution of disease and pest-free seeds, with the full cooperation of the Plant Quarantine Division of the Government of India.

EXCHANGE OF GERMPLASM

The success of international germplasm collection and utilization largely depends on its timely transfer and ease of mobility. Unfortunately, there are many hurdles that a germplasm sample has to pass through before it can reach its destination. From the plant quarantine point of view, it seems there is some tendency to overemphasize the risks involved in the exchange of germplasm. It is true that there is some risk in the transfer of unchecked germplasm from one region to another. It is also important to recognize that many samples may never reach their destination due to certain factors that may not be risky or are of low risk. The dilemma we are in is that many of these germplasm accessions can neither reach their destination nor survive for long in their original, threatened habitat.

It is beyond the scope of this chapter to list and discuss all the risks associated with germplasm exchange. The major diseases, pests, and weeds of importance for quarantine purposes are fairly well known (4, 7, 19). In general, it is well documented that many of the risks associated with germplasm transfer can be controlled. Khan (13) stated that the aim of plant quarantine is to prevent the introduction of harmful organisms to a new area. Likewise, it may be stated that the aim of germplasm collection and exchange is to conserve and introduce useful germplasm without

Table 5. Number of samples of ICRISAT crops received by the CPPTI during
1981 to 1982 compared with the number released and detained.

Crop	Number of samples imported	Samples released		Samples detained	
		No.	%	No.	%
Sorghum	1598	1313	82.2	285	17.8
Pearl millet	1450	1440	99.3	10	0.7
Pigeon pea	483	331	68.5	152	31.5
Chickpea	7	3	42.9	4	51.1
Groundnut	1342	963	71.8	379	28.2
Total	4880	4050	83.0	830	17.0

Source: Annual report, 1981 to 1982, Central Plant Protection and Training Institute,
Rajendranger, A.P., India.

endangering the new habitat. Therefore, there is something in common
between the two disciplines in that they both are necessary and useful.

At ICRISAT, several thousands of germplasm samples are exchanged
each year. Table 1 shows the total number of germplasm samples distributed from 1973 to 1983. All seeds that are exported or imported by
ICRISAT must pass through the Indian Government Plant Protection and
Quarantine Directorate. The Central Plant Protection Training Institute
(CPPTI) at Rajendranagar, Hyderbad, is a part of the Directorate of
Plant Protection responsible for the quarantine inspection and release of
all ICRISAT seeds. We are fortunate to have such an institute nearby and
grateful for their diligent handling and cooperation. In order to further
reduce the risk of importing and exporting diseases and pests to and from
India, ICRISAT has established a Post Entry Quarantine Isolation Area
(PEQIA) and an Export Plant Quarantine Laboratory, which functions in
close collaboration with the CPPTI. As an additional safety measure,
even after clearance from CPPTI, the imported seeds are sown in this
isolation area and scrutinized under the joint supervision of CPPTI and
ICRISAT staff during the entire period from germination to harvest. Dis-
eased and pest-infected plants are destroyed and seeds are collected only
from healthy plants.

It is reported by CPPTI (1) that a total of 4880 samples of ICRISAT
crops were processed by CPPTI for introduction during 1981 to 1982. The
cropwise breakdown and number of released and detained samples is
shown in Table 5. However, the number of samples released does not
always represent the actual number available at ICRISAT. For example,
a very large percentage of pearl millet samples have failed to germinate in
PEQIA. Although the CPPTI figure shows a 99.31% release of pearl
millet germplasm in 1981 to 1982, the actual percent of seeds that reached
the ICRISAT gene bank was much less than that. Out of 1121 pearl millet
samples that were introduced in 1981 to 1982 from six different countries,
1109 samples were released, of which 506 did not germinate. That means
that over 45% of the samples were lost. This is a very high loss of germplasm compared, for example, to an average of 2% detention of introduced seeds, screened at the North Central Regional Plant Introduction
Station in Ames, IA, as reported by Leppik (14).

The potential of a germplasm sample is largely unknown at the time
of collection. However, we have seen that a number of desirable

characters are identified whenever a diverse group of germplasm is evaluated and screened. At times, even those lines that show susceptibility to a disease or pest offer a rare source of breeding material for other agronomically desirable traits. For example, sorghum accessions IS-1082, 2122, 2145, 4663, 4664, 5470, 5484, 5566, 18551, and others have been identified as promising lines for shootfly resistance. However, they are susceptible to grain molds. Other sorghum germplasm lines such as IS-620, 621, 5959, 7237, 8219, 9308, 9482, and 11234 are promising lines for grain mold resistance; yet they are susceptible to shootfly and stem borer (*Hydraecia* sp.). Likewise in pigeon pea, ICP-7035 has multiple resistance to wilt and sterility mosaic, but it is susceptible to blight. ICP-7065 is resistant to blight, but highly susceptible to both wilt and sterility mosaic. There are many more examples like these which could have been rejected for one reason, while useful sources for their other traits.

In conclusion, plant quarantine is a very useful and necessary activity. A safe and rapid transfer of germplasm is vital for a sound crop improvement program. A great many exotic crops are flourishing in many areas of the world as a result of international transfer and exchange of germplasm. It is also true that new diseases and pests may be introduced with the germplasm into new areas. Nevertheless, import of small, experimental quantities of seeds with appropriate safeguards based on sound biological principles can often be an answer to improving the genetic base of crops. Much larger quantities of commercial seed often repeatedly enter a country with even greater quarantine risk but often with minimal or cursory inspection. Yet, germplasm is the basic raw material for future development of commercial seed and to impose undue restrictions on its movement appears to be an unnecessary and misguided practice.

Considering the worldwide crop improvement program and in view of the plant breeder's remarkable success in developing high yielding cultivars, it is obvious that there are significant advantages associated with international germplasm exchange. With careful handling, imaginative methods and more specific research on seed pathogen pest relationships, man should be able to save his valuable seeds.

ACKNOWLEDGMENTS

I wish to thank all my colleagues in the Genetic Resources Unit, and Dr. K. L. Mehra, director of National Bureau of Plant Genetic Resources, ICAR, New Delhi, India, for their assistance in reviewing and improving this paper. I also wish to express my appreciation to the CPPTI and ICRISAT Quarantine Unit for their assistance and cooperation.

REFERENCES

1. Central Plant Protection Training Institute. 1981–1982 Annual report. Rajendranagar, Hyderabad—500 030, A.P., India.
2. Chiarappa, L., and J. F. Karpati. 1981. Safe and rapid transfer of plant genetic resources: A proposal for a global system. FAO/UNEP/IBPGR Technical conference on Crop Genetic Resources. AGP: 1981/M/6, FAO, Rome.

3. Cocking, M. R. et al. 1981. Aspects of plant genetic manipulation. Nature 293(5830): 265–270.

4. Gonzalez, H. R. 1977. Entomological. p. 25–28. *In* W. B. Hewitt and L. Chiarappa (ed.) Plant quarantine in international transfer of genetic resources. CRC Press, Boca Raton, FL.

5. Harlan, J. R. 1975. Crops and man. American Society of Agronomy, and Crop Science Society of America, Madison, WI.

6. Hawkes, J. G. 1981. Germplasm collection, preservation and use. p. 57–83. *In* K. J. Frey (ed.) Plant breeding II. Iowa State University Press, Ames.

7. Hewitt, W. B. 1977. Pathological. p. 3–16. *In* W. B. Hewitt and L. Chiarappa (ed.) Plant quarantine in international transfer of genetic resources. CRC Press, Boca Raton, IL.

8. ICRISAT. 1980. Annual report. Genetic Resources Unit, ICRISAT, Patancheru, A.P., India. p. 253–259.

9. ––––. 1981. Annual report. Genetic Resources Unit, ICRISAT, Patancheru, A.P. India. p. 16–18.

10. International Board for Plant Genetic Resources. 1979. Seed technology for gene banks. AGP: IBPGR/79/31. IBPGR Secretariat, Rome.

11. Jain, H. K. 1982. Plant breeders' rights and genetic resources. Indian J. Genet. 42:121–128.

12. Justice, O. L., and L. N. Bass. 1978. Principles and practices of seed storage. USDA—Agriculture Handb. no. 506. U.S. Government Printing Office, Washington, DC.

13. Khan, R. P. 1977. Plant quarantine: Principles, methodology, and suggested approaches. p. 289–308. *In* W. B. Kewitt and L. Chiarappa (ed.) Plant health and quarantine in international transfer of genetic resources. CRS Press, Boca Raton, FL.

14. Leppik, E. E. 1969. List of foreign pests, pathogens, and weeds detected on introduced plants. Plant Introduction Paper no. 15, Beltsville, MD.

15. Maude, R. B. 1973. Seed-borne diseases and their control. p. 325–335. *In* W. Heydecker (ed.) Seed ecology. Butterworths, Massachusetts.

16. Mehra, K. L., and R. K. Arora. 1982. Plant genetic resources of India—their diversity and conservation. Indian Council of Agricultural Research, National Bureau of Plant Genetic Resources, New Delhi.

17. Mengesha, M. H., and K. E. Prasada Rao. 1981. Current situation and future of sorghum germplasm. p. 323–333. *In* Sorghum in the eighties; Proc. of the Int. Symposium on Sorghum. 2–7 November. ICRISAT, Patancheru, A.P., India.

18. ––––. 1982. World sorghum germplasm collection and conservation. A paper approved for publication as C.P. No. 141, ICRISAT, Patancheru, A.P., India.

19. Naidu, P. H., and K. K. Nirula. 1979. Quarantine important diseases of sorghum, pearl millet, chickpea, pigeonpea and groundnut. Indian J. Plant Protection VII(2):175–188.

20. Roberts, E. H. 1974. Viability of seeds. Chapman and Hall Ltd., London.

21. Saxena, N. P., and A. R. Sheldrake. 1979. Physiology of growth, development, and yield of chickpeas in India. p. 106–120. *In* Proc. of the Int. workshop on Chickpea Improvement. 28 February–2 March. ICRISAT, Patancheru, A.P., India.

Chapter 6

Germplasm Preservation[1]

LOUIS N. BASS[2]

GERMPLASM RESOURCES

Crop germplasm resources may be defined as the total array of living species, subspecies, and their genetic variants, which are, or may be, important to humanity's present and future welfare. There are many aspects of designing, constructing, and developing a gene bank, such as design criteria, location, reliability of the power supply, etc., which could be discussed but are outside the scope of this presentation. This discussion will be limited to preservation of germplasm resources, whether in a natural state or under controlled conditions. Perpetuation of species in their natural habitat is, of course, highly desirable but not always either practical or possible. Preservation of the total array of crop germplasm is a broad and difficult task. Although most discussions on germplasm preservation have been centered around crops such as corn (*Zea mays* L.), wheat (*Triticum* spp. L.), rice (*Oryza sativa* L.), sorghum [*Sorghum bicolor* (L.) Moench], cotton (*Gossypium* spp. L.), and other major industrial crops, numerous other species are also important to preserve.

PRESERVATION METHODS

In its broadest sense, preservation includes controlled environment storage of seeds and other plant propagules and maintenance of living plants, either under controlled conditions or as natural stands. Because

---

[1] Contribution of the National Seed Storage Lab., Fort Collins, CO 80523.
[2] Research plant physiologist, USDA-ARS, National Seed Storage Laboratory, Fort Collins, CO 80523.

Copyright © 1984 Crop Science Society of America, 677 South Segoe Road, Madison, WI 53711. *Conservation of Crop Germplasm—An International Perspective.*

the USA has no native germplasm of the major crops, except sunflower (*Helianthus annuus* L.), and has to depend upon other countries for native or wild germplasm; it is not directly involved in a major way in the development or setting aside of natural areas for perpetuation of crop species and their wild relatives in their native environment. The USA is, however, involved formally in preserving some introduced crop germplasm as living plants in clonal repositories and informally in arboreta, nurseries, and botanic gardens. Some native germplasm is maintained in forest preserves, wild areas, prairie preserves, etc. However, most germplasm in the USA, especially that of the major crops, is preserved as viable seeds stored under controlled environmental conditions.

Several publications discuss broad aspects of gene resources, genetic vulnerability, and germplasm conservation (James, 1967; Frankel and Bennett, 1970; National Academy of Sciences, 1972, 1978; Frankel and Hawkes, 1975; International Board of Plant Genetics Resources, 1975; Matsuo, 1975; Hawkes et al., 1976; Frankel and Soule, 1981).

The present value of germplasm preservation facilities may not be immediately apparent, but as time goes on they will become increasingly important. Modern improved varieties are gradually encroaching on centers of crop origins so that pockets where disease and/or insect resistance are found are becoming more and more confined. If materials from these pockets are not collected and preserved, they will be lost forever to plant breeders. By placing such germplasm in appropriate preservation facilities, they will be available to plant breeders indefinitely. One preserved valuable plant germplasm accession may later save an agricultural industry; thus, the benefits realized from one germplasm accession could conceivably pay for the construction of good preservation facilities and the cost of maintaining them for many years.

The international interest in the genetic diversity of plants of actual and potential use by humans principally for food, fiber, forage, and oil relates to the identification of geographic centers of genetic diversity on which much plant exploration has been based. The present world situation makes it necessary for plant breeders and other scientists to intensify their efforts toward solution of the eventual population/food confrontation. This will, no doubt, require new genetic inputs to solve the problems associated with expanded production under less than ideal environmental conditions.

SOURCES OF GENETIC DIVERSITY

Gaps still exist in the available base of genetic diversity. Sources having the greatest potential for genetic diversity include wild populations of crop species, wild relatives of cultivated species, and primitive varieties that often contain genes for disease and insect resistance. As mentioned earlier, these resources are being rapidly depleted, displaced, or abandoned. Therefore, there is a great urgency to identify the gaps in our genetic diversity and make the necessary collections to fill them. Other sources of genetic diversity include obsolete cultivars, current cultivars, breeding lines, breeding stocks, and elite germplasm which also need to be systematically collected and preserved. The very nature of collecting and preserving crop genetic resources requires international cooperation (National Academy of Sciences, 1972).

TYPES OF GERMPLASM COLLECTIONS

The International Board for Plant Genetics Resources (IBPGR) classifies assemblages of genetic resources as base, active, and duplicate collections (IBPGR, 1976; Cromarty et al., 1982). Base collections are intended for long-term preservation and may be comprised of: (a) substantial collections of a wide range of species; (b) substantial collections of a limited range of species; (c) significant and original special purpose collections; and (d) replicates of any or all of these. Active or working col- used for multiplication, evaluation, documentation, distribution, and use by plant breeders. Duplicate collections are duplicates of base collections that are housed in a geographically different location for security purposes.

To further that cooperation, IBPGR has played a central role in the organization of a worldwide network of genetic resources centers. Certain important conservation centers have been asked to accept responsibility for storage of major base collections, either on a world or regional basis. Other centers have been asked to provide storage for duplicate collections of germplasm of the major crops and their wild relatives.

INTERNATIONAL NETWORK OF GERMPLASM PRESERVATION CENTERS

International Research Centers

International centers which have agreed to serve as world or regional depositories for base collections for the crops they are working with include: Centro Internacional de Agricultura Tropical (CIAT), Columbia, bean (*Phaseolus* spp. L.); Centro Internacional de la Papa (CIP), Peru, potato (*Solanum tuberosum* L.); International Crops Research Institute for the Semi-Arid Tropics (ICRISAT), India, millet [*Panicum miliaceum* L., *Pennisetum americanum* (L.) Leeke, and *Eleusine coracana* (L.) Gaertn.], pigeon pea [*Cajanus cajan* (L.) Huth], chickpea (*Cicer arietinum* L.), and peanut (*Arachis hypogaea* L.); International Institute of Tropical Agriculture (IITA), Nigeria, African rice (*Oryza glaberrima* Steud.) and cowpea [*Vigna unguiculata* (L.) Walp.]; and International Rice Research Institute (IRRI), Philippines, rice (*Oryza sativa* L.). The International Center for Agricultural Research in Dry Areas (ICARDA), Syria, has agreed to serve in a world capacity for its priority crops when adequate storage facilities have been established (IBPGR, 1982).

National/Regional Centers

By the end of 1982, national/regional centers in Argentina, Belgium, Canada, Costa Rica, Ethiopia, German Democratic Republic, German Federal Republic, Greece, India, Italy, Japan, Netherlands, Nigeria, Philippines, Poland, Portugal, Spain, Sweden, Thailand, United Kingdom, USA, and USSR were participating in the IBPGR network of base centers for crop germplasm (IBPGR, 1982).

Other Centers

Germplasm is also preserved at various research institutes, universities, botanic gardens, arboreta, nurseries, and even in private collections. However, germplasm in private collections is frequently difficult to locate. Worldwide, more than 36 countries are active in the preservation of genetic diversity through maintenance of germplasm collections of one or more crops. As of 1979, more than 75 centers had or were constructing seed storage facilities. No estimate was available for the number of centers preserving vegetatively propagated germplasm (Ng and Williams, 1979). No estimate is available for the number of germplasm preservation centers planned or completed since 1979.

UNITED STATES NATIONAL PLANT GERMPLASM SYSTEM

Plants from which the USA derives most of its food and fiber were introduced from other countries because only a few crop plants are native. With very little native crop germplasm and a shallow base of primitive cultivars, modern agriculture in the USA depends upon a coordinated system to introduce, evaluate, distribute, and preserve the germplasm obtained from throughout the world. Furthermore, the complexity of modern plant research demands an efficiently organized effort to assure that plant breeders get the germplasm they need. No one local institution can be expected to provide the germplasm required by the array of breeders working with even a single crop.

In the USA, the National Plant Germplasm System (NPGS) is a coordinated network of Federal, State, and private sector institutions, agencies, and research units which work cooperatively to introduce, maintain, evaluate, catalog, and distribute all types of plant germplasm. Primary financial and administrative support for the components of the system comes from the Agricultural Research Service (ARS) of the U.S. Department of Agriculture (USDA) and from the State Agricultural Experiment Stations (SAES). Commercial plant breeders, seed trade interests, and private citizens also contribute to and support the system.

The mission of these cooperative units is to provide plant scientists, now and in the future, with the germplasm needed to carry out their research. The research programs thus supported are widely varied. They include breeding new cultivars for increased yield and quality, for ease of harvesting, better processing and longer storage; for resistance to diseases, insects, mechanical damage, temperature extremes, unfavorable soil moisture, salinity, smog, and other environmental stresses; for erosion control, beautification, noise abatement, and resistance to fire; and as sources of medicinal and industrial chemicals. The quality of operation of the system, under its funding constraints, is evidenced by the reasonably good status of our crop genetic resources.

The NPGS (Anonymous, 1981) seeks to contribute to the stability of the agriculture of the USA and of the world, to enhance its development, and to provide it with new vistas by fulfilling the expressed and continuing needs of research workers for plant germplasm drawn from worldwide resources. The primary components of the NPGS are the Regional Plant Introduction Stations, special curators, clonal repositories, and the USDA-ARS-National Seed Storage Laboratory (NSSL).

Regional Plant Introduction Stations

The Regional Plant Introduction Stations are charged with the responsibility for introduction, multiplication, distribution, preservation, and evaluation of seed propagated plants for industrial and agricultural utilization. The Coordinators of the Regional Plant Introduction Stations are the curators of the working collections which plant scientists draw upon for their day-to-day germplasm needs of most crop species. There are special problems associated with the wide range of plant materials the Regional Plant Introduction Stations must maintain. Each species has its own requirements for optimum growth and seed production. Some species require special pollination, while others are self-pollinated. Seed must be carefully dried to a safe level for storage at a temperature of around 5°C and 35 to 40% relative humidity (RH). Because of the need for frequent access to the seed samples, they cannot be stored in hermetically sealed containers.

Special Curators

Within the NPGS special curators are used for certain large collections such as cotton (*Gossypium* spp. L.), flax (*Linum usitatissimum* L.), soybean [*Glycine max* (L.) Merr.]; and small grains (*Avena* spp. L., *Hordeum vulgare* L., *Triticum* spp. L., *Secale cereale* L., X *Triticosecale*, and *Oryza sativa* L.), among others.

Clonal Repositories

Several clonal repositories, some of which are in operation, are being developed for preservation of vegetatively propagated crops such as pears (*Pyrus* spp. L.), stone fruits (*Prunus* spp. L.), hops (*Humulus* spp. L.), mints (*Mentha* spp. L.), citrus (*Citrus* spp. L.), grapes (*Vitis* spp. L.), dates (*Phoenix dactylifera* L.), apples (*Malus* spp. Mill.), berries (*Fragaria* spp. L., *Rubus* spp. L.), and filberts (*Corylus* spp. L.), etc. The Regional Plant Introduction Stations also maintain a limited amount of vegetatively propagated germplasm.

The National Seed Storage Laboratory

A cooperative relationship exists between the Regional Stations, other germplasm curators, and the NSSL. Duplicate samples of seed of all plant introductions and other seed propagated germplasm are sent to the

NSSL for safe, long-term, backup storage, and maintenance. Types of germplasm which are submitted for storage include all introductions, current and obsolete cultivars, inbred lines, some genetic stocks, and any other germplasm stocks considered worthy of long-term preservation in the base collection.

Because the NSSL is considered to be a long-term or base storage facility, seed from it is not furnished to scientists unless there is no other source.

Storage conditions in the NSSL are maintained at about −18°C with the seeds stored in sealed, moisture-barrier packages after having been dried to 5 or 6% moisture content. Seed of each accession is tested for viability before being placed in long-term storage. Subsequently, a 5-year germination retest program is followed. When seed viability drops to a predetermined level, arrangements are made for production of a new generation with as near as possible the same genetic composition as the original accession.

In addition to the Regional Plant Introduction Stations, the special curators, the clonal repositories, and the NSSL, which constitutes the NPGS; there are many other collections of plant germplasm in the USA being maintained by commercial plant breeders, colleges and universities, other government agencies, botanic gardens, and other responsible parties. The majority of these would be considered to be working collections with those outside the NPGS having no responsibility for either maintaining or distributing germplasm.

SEED STORAGE BEHAVIOR

Most seeds can be classified as either orthodox or recalcitrant according to their response to desiccation.

Orthodox Seeds

Orthodox seeds can be dried to a low moisture content (3 to 5%) with little or no loss of viability. For most orthodox seeds, the lower the seed moisture content and the lower the storage temperature, within certain limits, the greater the longevity. A majority of crop seeds are orthodox.

Recalcitrant Seeds

Recalcitrant seeds cannot ordinarily be dried below certain critical species specific moisture contents without a rapid loss of viability.

LONG-TERM STORAGE REQUIREMENTS

Orthodox Seeds

The conditions recommended by IBPGR for storage of base collections are probably most suitable and economical to maintain by conventional mechanical refrigeration methods (Justice and Bass, 1978; Bass, 1980; Cromarty et al., 1982). The preferred standard for base seed collections is storage at 5% seed moisture content in sealed, moisture-proof containers at −18°C or colder.

Seed moisture content during storage can be controlled either by predrying to about 5% before sealing in a moisture-proof container or by storage in an adequately dehumidified atmosphere. At −18°C an RH of 10 to 15% is required to maintain 5% seed moisture content. Because of the cost of dehydration of the storage area, it is more economical to use hermetically sealed containers. Also, if the refrigeration or dehumidification equipment should fail, seeds in open storage could gradually increase in moisture content to an unsafe level while seeds in moisture-proof containers would not (Justice and Bass, 1978; Cromarty et al., 1982).

Under certain circumstances a temperature of −10°C may be acceptable for long-term storage of certain species (Cromarty et al., 1982). However, such storage could significantly increase the frequency of regeneration and thus result in greater opportunity for loss of genetic diversity and increasing preservation costs.

For seeds with inherently poor keeping qualities, it may be advisable to use either a seed moisture content lower than 5%, a temperature colder than −18°C, or both. However, seed of some species may be damaged by either too much dehydration or too cold a temperature. These points must be verified for each species before very low seed moisture contents and very cold temperatures are used for routine storage of germplasm samples (Bass, 1973, 1979, 1980a, 1980b; 1981).

Research in progress at the NSSL has demonstrated that seeds of numerous crops that are air-dried under ambient laboratory temperature and RH conditions (approximately 20°C and 35% RH) can be subjected to freezing at −196°C, the temperature of liquid N (LN$_2$), and subsequent rewarming with no adverse effects on germination (Stanwood and Bass, 1978, 1981; Stanwood and Roos, 1979; Stanwood, 1980).

In a long-term study (50 plus years) involving a large number of genera, species, and cultivars of field crop, vegetable, and flower seeds, tests after 3 years storage showed that, for the kinds of seeds included, storage at −196°C (cryogenic storage) had no adverse effect on germination.

Typically, an LN$_2$ storage container has a double wall with a vacuum between the walls to provide maximum insulation for the LN$_2$ which is at normal atmospheric pressure. Seeds can be stored within the liquid or in the vapor above the liquid. Seeds in the liquid will be held at −196°C and seeds in the vapor will be at a temperature of around −150°C.

There are advantages and disadvantages with regard to both conventional or cryogenic storage. Probably the most significant advantages of conventional storage are storage capacity and storage environment, both of which favorably impact sample size, and ease of retrieval. The most significant advantages of cryogenic storage are that no electrical equipment is needed and the expected much longer storage life. However, just as conventional storage methods require a dependable source of electricity, cryogenic storage requires a dependable source of liquid N.

The NSSL is doing research on the possible use of liquid N as a storage refrigerant for base collections of germplasm. However, these studies have not been under way long enough to determine the long-term effects of storage in LN_2 on either seed longevity or genetic stability. In cooperation with Colorado State University, the NSSL has initiated a project to study the cytogenetic effects of cryogenic storage on seeds of barley (*Hordeum vulgare* L.) and other species.

Recalcitrant Seeds

Recalcitrant seeded species include many important tropical crops (coffee, cocoa, rubber, and anthurium), as well as some temperate crops (wild rice, oak, and walnut). Using presently accepted storage practices, recalcitrant seeds cannot be preserved for long periods of time. Consequently, until satisfactory long-term seed storage methods are developed for recalcitrant seeds, the species involved will have to be preserved by cell or tissue culture or in clonal repositories (King and Roberts, 1979; Chin and Roberts, 1980). Preliminary results of research in the NSSL indicate that cryogenic storage may have a place in the long-term preservation of recalcitrant seeds and vegetative propagules once techniques are refined.

SHORT-TERM STORAGE REQUIREMENTS

Orthodox Seeds

Storage temperature requirements are usually not as low for working collections as for base collections because of their higher rate of usage and resultant more frequent need for multiplication. Also, with working collections people frequently have to spend long periods in the storage room putting up samples for distribution. Therefore, employee comfort is of considerable importance. Seed samples in working collections are stored in various types of containers such as cloth or paper bags, metal cans, or glass jars. Glass jars, although fragile, provide easy visual access to the quantity of seed remaining in a sample. Both screw cap glass jars and metal cans provide easy access to the seeds for sample removal. A temperature of 5°C and an RH of 35 to 40% is adequate for most orthodox species for from 5 to 25 years.

Recalcitrant Seeds

Recalcitrant seeds are susceptible to such things as desiccation damage, chilling injury, attack by fungi, and germination during storage. Consequently, it is not possible to store most recalcitrant seeds for more than a few days, weeks, or at best, months. Even for these short periods of storage, extreme care must be taken in selecting the storage temperature and RH. Some species can tolerate a moderately low temperature while others must be kept at a moderately warm temperature. Some kinds of seeds formerly throught to be recalcitrant have recently been found to remain viable when dried to a low moisture content. Perhaps other apparently recalcitrant seeds can also be dried without damage. It is clear that more research is needed on safe storage of recalcitrant seeds.

DRYING METHODS

To attain the required moisture content for hermetic storage, seeds must be either mechanically or chemically dried. For best results mechanical drying should be done in a forced, heated air dryer at a temperature no higher than 38°C for a prescribed time dependent upon the kind of seed being dried. For chemical drying, either an appropriate amount of a suitable desiccant can be put into an hermetically sealed container, to bring the seeds in the container to the desired moisture content, or a desiccant dehumidifier can be used to adjust the RH to an appropriate level (usually about 10 to 15%) in a drying room maintained at about 15°C with good air circulation (Justice and Bass, 1978; Cromarty et al., 1982). The possibilities of using freeze drying for preparing germplasm samples for storage has received little attention.

PACKAGING

Glass, metal, or heatsealable aluminum-foil laminates are frequently used as containers for hermetic storage of seeds. Glass containers provide excellent moisture protection; however, they are fragile and some types are frequently difficult to seal. Metal cans are not fragile and are easy to seal with rather inexpensive sealing equipment. However, most cans, except those usually used for paint, have the disadvantage of having to be discarded after opening as they cannot be resealed. Heatsealable aluminum-foil laminate containers have the advantages of low cost, recloseability, and more efficient use of storage space. Such containers can usually be opened and resealed several times before having to be replaced. For storage at a controlled RH, seeds can be packaged in either a paper or cloth container. Moisture content of seeds in such containers adjust quite rapidly to changes in RH and/or temperature in the storage room. Consequently, seed in cloth or paper containers are less likely to be damaged by rapid changes in storage environment than are seed in moisture resistant packages. Packaging in polyethylene or other moisture resistant material is not recommended for either hermetic or controlled atmosphere storage of germplasm samples. Thin gauges of polyethylene and other similar materials are moisture resistant, not moisture proof. Therefore, seeds packaged in sealed containers of such material and held under high RH conditions can increase in moisture content to a level that would be unsafe if accidentally exposed to too high a temperature. Moisture content of seeds sealed in such containers gradually increases or decreases with changes in RH of the storage area. Changes in storage temperature can also cause seed moisture content to increase or decrease, but seed moisture content changes may not be rapid enough to prevent damage to seed viability when exposed to relatively high temperatures. Thick gauges, 10 to 15 mil of polyethylene and similar materials afford better moisture protection than thin gauges, but even these materials are not moisture proof. Use of such materials can give germplasm curators a false sense of security unless they are aware of the shortcomings of most plastic materials (Bass et al., 1961; Justice and Bass, 1978; Cromarty et al., 1982).

SAMPLE SIZE

There is no universal agreement on what constitutes an adequate sample. The IBPGR (1976) recommends that the initial size of each accession in a base collection should, if possible, not be less than 4000 seeds for genetically uniform material and 12 000 seeds for heterogeneous material, and that 1000 and 3000 seeds, respectively, be in duplicate collections in other centers. It is also suggested that for very large seeds these quantities may need to be reduced. For working collections the sample should be large enough to meet demand without regeneration for a minimum of 5 and, preferably, 10 years.

When considering what constitutes an adequate sample, factors such as available storage space, cost of constructing additional storage space if and when needed, time in storage, germination retest intervals, number of seeds per germination test, possible distribution frequency, and number of seeds distributed per request have to be taken into account.

Although a 4 × 100-seed germination test is required for labeling of seed for commercial sale, it is not necessary to use that many seeds for viability monitoring of germplasm samples. Because of wide variations that occur in the distribution of weak and dead seeds within samples of many kinds of seeds, it is, however, recommended that a 2 × 100-seed germination test be used whenever possible.

For small samples of kinds which usually germinate uniformly, a 50-, 25-, or even 20-seed germination test would provide some indication of the viability of the seed lot, but would not provide a measure of variability within the lot. Generally, the smaller the number of seed germinated, the greater the possibility of obtaining inaccurate test results. Ellis et al. (1980) have suggested that gene banks adopt a sequential test procedure for monitoring viability of germplasm accessions. Briefly, the sequential germination test procedure suggested is as follows: Germinate a random sample of 40 seeds, if the germination percentage is satisfactory, store or retain in storage; if unsatisfactory, regenerate as soon as possible; if inconclusive, continue the sequential test and use the accumulated germination results to determine when to regenerate. A sequential test, although good in theory, could in practice double the work involved in preparing each sample for storage.

At the NSSL, although it is preferable to start out with a minimum of 10 000 seeds in each accession, the following minimum quantities have been established in cooperation with the appropriate committees of the Crop Science Society of America: 10 000 seeds for small-seeded, 5000 seeds for large-seeded species and cultivars, and 500 seeds for parental and germplasm lines and difficult to produce kinds. It is understood that the curators of the active collections are responsible for maintaining and distributing germplasm to users, and that the sample in the NSSL will be replaced from time to time by the curator of the active collection to assure that viable seeds are continuously in reserve.

The quantity of seed stored should permit periodic monitoring of viability and provide seed for regeneration and distribution when necessary.

The normal germination retest interval used in the NSSL is 5 years; however, a few species known to be long lived are retested on a 10-year schedule. As experience is gained, it may be possible to lengthen the time between germination tests for additional species. In a gene bank, it is not possible to monitor viability by using a composite sample of a species because of differences in seed longevity among cultivars and accessions. Every accession must be individually monitored to guard against loss caused by an especially rapid rate of decline in viability.

OBJECTIVES OF A BASE COLLECTION

The primary objective of a base collection is to preserve indefinitely specific germplasm accessions in order to maintain as broad a germplasm base as possible for the future. Another objective of a base collection is to reduce the risk of genetic changes introduced through frequent regeneration. Storing too few seeds could increase the frequency of regeneration resulting from depletion of the seed supply, rather than from loss of viability; and, thus increase the possibility of change in the genetic composition of a germplasm line through accidental means during regeneration, such a cross-pollination, mechanical mixtures, and other similar causes.

Another objective is to prevent genetic changes in the stored germplasm accessions resulting from excessive deterioration (Roos, 1982). Scientists agree that the frequency of chromosome aberrations in root tips increases with declining viability and vigor, but there is not universal agreement among scientists as to the effect, if any, of these root tip chromosomal aberrations upon the genetic characteristics of plants and seeds produced in subsequent generations. Studies conducted at the NSSL (Murata et al., 1977, 1980, 1981, 1982) indicate that with continued growth of a plant, chromosomal aberrations observed in root tips at first mitosis are eliminated and have no effect upon genetic characteristics of subsequent generations.

Major concerns of curators of both base and working collections are how many seeds should be planted, how many plants should be pollinated, and how many plants should be harvested for seed for regeneration to assure that all genetic diversity included in the initial seed sample is adequately maintained. Factors such as pollination control for inbred lines and cross-pollinated species, disease, insect, and weather related damage, among others, are also of great concern. These are of greater concern for heterogeneous accessions than for homogeneous accessions. As seed lots deteriorate, there is some natural selection for seed longevity because some genotypes normally lose viability more rapidly than others and some genotypes produce more seeds than others. When rapid loss of viability is associated with low seed production, the progeny from a field planting soon shows a marked decrease in the percentage of some genotypes. A corresponding marked increase in the percentage of other genotypes will occur unless special precautions are taken to assure that each genotype will be present in the progeny of a regeneration planting in the same ratio as in the original seed sample (Roos, 1977).

There is always a possibility of having to plant seed of a given accession more than one time to accomplish successful multiplication; therefore, adequate seeds must be retained for at least two or three multiplication plantings.

SUMMARY

Preservation of crop germplasm is important to future agricultural development. To meet the needs of plant breeders and other plant scientists, it is necessary to preserve as broad a germplasm base as possible. To prevent as much as possible the occurrence of genetic change during preservation, seed storage conditions must reduce the rate of viability loss to the lowest possible level. Regeneration must be accomplished on a timely basis using growing procedures that will assure the continued availability in the same relative proportions of all components of a heterogeneous germplasm accession with a minimum amount of genetic change.

Cryogenic storage could be a valuable preservation method in the future, especially for small seeds and those that are difficult to produce. There is also a possibility that cryogenic storage may be useful in preservation of recalcitrant seeds and other plant propagules, however, much research is needed before routine use of these technologies can become a reality.

REFERENCES

1. Anonymous. 1981. The national plant germplasm system. Science and Education, USDA, Washington, DC.

2. Bass, L. N. 1973. Controlled atmosphere and seed storage. USDA Seed Quality Research Symposium 1971:463–492.

3. ————. 1979. Physiological aspects of seed preservation. p. 145–170. *In* I. Rubenstein and R. L. Phillips (ed.) The plant seed: Development, preservation, and germination. Academic Press, New York.

4. ————. 1980a. Principles of seed storage. Modern Government/National Development. p. 60–64; 67–69; 72–73.

5. ————. 1980b. Seed viability during long-term storage. p. 117–141. *In* Jules Janick (ed.) Horticultural review. Vol. 2. AVI Publishing Co., Westport, CT.

6. ————. 1981. Storage conditions for maintaining seed quality. p. 239–321. *In* E. E. Finney, Jr. (ed.) Handbook of transportation and marketing in agriculture, Vol. II, Field Crops. CRC Press, Boca Raton, FL.

7. ————, Te May Ching, and F. L. Winter. 1961. Packages that protect seeds. *In* USDA Yearbook of Agriculture, "Seeds":330–338.

8. Chin, H. F., and E. H. Roberts. 1980. Recalcitrant crop seeds. Tropical Press SDN. BHD.

9. Cromarty, A. S., R. H. Ellis, and E. H. Roberts. 1982. The design of seed storage facilities for genetic conservation. IBPGR Secretariat, Rome.

10. Ellis, R. H., E. H. Roberts, and J. Whitehead. 1980. A new, more economic and accurate approach to monitoring the viability of accessions during storage in seed banks. Plant genetic resources—Newsl. 41. IBPGR, Rome, Italy.

11. Frankel, O. H., and E. Bennett. 1970. Genetic resources in plants—Their exploration and conservation. Handb. no. 11. Blackwell Scientific Publications, Oxford.

12. ————, and J. G. Hawkes. 1975. Crop genetic resources for today and tomorrow. International Biological Programme 2. Cambridge University Press, New York.

13. ————, and Soule. 1981. Conservation and evolution. Cambridge University Press, New York.

14. Hawkes, J. G., J. T. Williams, and Jean Hanson. 1976. A bibliography of plant genetic resources. IBPGR Secretariat, Rome.

15. International Board of Plant Genetics Resources. 1975. The conservation of crop genetic resources. The Whitefriars Press Ltd., London.

16. ————. 1976. Report of the working group on engineering, design and cost aspects of long-term seed storage facilities. IBPGR, Rome.

17. ————. 1982. Annual report. IBPGR Secretariat, Rome.

18. James, E. 1967. Preservation of seed stocks. Adv. Agron. 19:87–106.

19. Justice, O. L., and L. N. Bass. 1978. Principles and practices of seed storage. Agriculture Handb. no. 506. (Reprinted, Castle House, England 1979).

20. King, M. W., and E. H. Roberts. 1979. The storage of recalcitrant seeds—achievements and possible approaches. IBPGR Secretariat.

21. Matsuo, T. 1975. Gene conservation—Exploration, collection, preservation and utilization of genetic resources. JIBP Synthesis. Vol. 5. Univ. of Tokyo Press, Tokyo.

22. Murata, M., E. E. Roos, and T. Tsuchiya. 1977. Analysis of the first mitotic divisions in germinating seeds of barley. Barley Genet. Newsl. 7:81–84.

23. ————, ————, and ————. 1980. Mitotic delay in root tips of peas induced by artificial seed aging. Bot. Gaz. 141(1):19–23.

24. ————, ————, and ————. 1981. Chromosome damage induced by artificial seed aging in barley. I. Germinability and frequency of aberrant anaphases at first mitosis. Can. J. Genet. Cytol. 23:267–280.

25. ————, T. Tsuchiya, and E. E. Roos. 1982. Chromosome damage induced by artificial seed aging in barley. II. Types of chromosomal aberrations at first mitosis. Bot. Gaz. 143(1):111–116.

26. National Academy of Sciences. 1972. Genetic vulnerability of major crops. National Academy of Sciences, Washington, DC.

27. ————. 1978. Conservation of germplasm resources—An imperative. National Academy of Sciences, Washington, DC.

28. Ng, N. Q., and J. T. Williams. 1979. Seed stores for genetic conservation. IBPGR, Rome.

29. Roos, E. E. 1977. Genetic shifts in bean populations during germplasm preservation. Annu. Rep. Bean Improv. Coop. 20:47–49.

30. ————. 1982. Induced genetic changes in seed germplasm during storage. p. 409–434. In A. A. Khan (ed.) The physiology and biochemistry of seed development, dormancy, and germination.

31. Stanwood, P. C. 1980. Tolerance of crop seeds to cooling and storage in liquid nitrogen (−196°C). J. Seed Technol. 5(1):26–31.

32. ————, and L. N. Bass. 1978. Ultracold preservation of seed germplasm. p. 361–371. In P. Li and A. Sakai (ed.) Plant cold hardiness and freezing stress. Academic Press, New York.

33. ————, and ————. 1981. Seed germplasm preservation using liquid nitrogen. Seed Sci. Technol. 9:423–437.

34. ————, and E. E. Roos. 1979. Seed storage of several horticultural species in liquid nitrogen (−196°C). HortScience 14(5):628–630.